CO 1 57 11048 X3

CW00435205

THE GOVERNMENT
and the
ECONOMY

access to politics

THE GOVERNMENT
and the
ECONOMY

Adrian Lyons

Series Editor: David Simpson

DURHAM CO ARTS LIBRARIES & MUSEUMS	
5711048	
	13.7.99
330.942	£6.50

Hodder & Stoughton

A MEMBER OF THE HODDER HEADLINE GROUP

DEDICATION

To Professor Anthony King of the University of Essex, whose infectious enthusiasm for the study of government and politics inspired me.

ACKNOWLEDGEMENTS

The publishers would like to thank the following for granting permission to reproduce photographs:

Saatchi & Saatchi: page 53; Rover Group UK Press Office: page 75; European Parliament: page 87; PA News: page 101.

Orders: please contact Bookpoint Ltd, 39 Milton Park, Abingdon, Oxon OX14 4TD. Telephone: (44) 01235 400414, Fax: (44) 01235 400454. Lines are open from 9.00–6.00, Monday to Saturday, with a 24 hour message answering service. Email address: orders@bookpoint.co.uk

A catalogue record for this title is available from The British Library

ISBN 0 340 74278X

First published 1999
Impression number 10 9 8 7 6 5 4 3 2 1
Year   2004 2003 2002 2001 2000 1999

Copyright © 1999, Adrian Lyons

All rights reserved. No part of this publication may be reproduced or transmitted in any form or by any means, electronic or mechanical, including photocopy, recording, or any information storage and retrieval system, without permission in writing from the publisher or under licence from the Copyright Licensing Agency Limited. Further details of such licences (for reprographic reproduction) may be obtained from the Copyright Licensing Agency Limited, of 90 Tottenham Court Road, London W1P 9HE.

Typeset by Transet Limited, Coventry, England.
Printed in Great Britain for Hodder & Stoughton Educational, a division of Hodder Headline plc, 338 Euston Road, London NW1 3BH by Redwood Books, Trowbridge, Wilts.

CONTENTS

PREFACE

A/AS Level syllabuses in Government and Politics aim to develop knowledge and understanding of the political system of the UK. They cover its local, national and European Union dimensions, and include comparative studies of aspects of other political systems, in order to ensure an understanding of the distinctive nature of the British political system. The minimum requirements for comparative study are aspects of systems with a separation of powers, how other systems protect the rights of individuals and how other electoral systems work.

Access to Politics is a series of concise topic books which cover the syllabus requirements, providing students with the necessary resources to complete the course successfully.

General advice on approaching exam questions

To achieve high grades you need to demonstrate consistency. Clearly address all parts of a question, make good use of essay plans or notes, and plan your time to cover all the questions.

Make your answers stand out from the crowd by using contemporary material to illustrate them. You should read a quality newspaper and listen to or watch appropriate programmes on radio and television.

Skills Advice

You should comprehend, synthesise and interpret political information in a variety of forms:

- Analyse and evaluate political institutions, processes and behaviour, political arguments and explanations.
- Identify parallels, connections, similarities and differences between aspects of the political systems studied.
- Select and organise relevant material to construct arguments and explanations leading to reasoned conclusions.
- Communicate the arguments with relevance, clarity and coherence, using vocabulary appropriate to the study of Government and Politics.

David Simpson

1

INTRODUCTION

ANTHONY KING, PROFESSOR of Government at the University of Essex and one of Britain's leading political commentators, has often expressed the view that politics and economics are two sides of the same coin. This is particularly true in Britain where general elections are usually dominated by the issue of the economy. While many areas of the Government and Politics syllabus are interesting and important, it is the public perception of government and the economy that has most bearing on the popularity of the government and therefore on its chances of re-election.

Just what questions are 'economic' is difficult to determine. Look at these news headlines taken from one newspaper's front page on one ordinary day in 1998, and try to decide which stories are to do with economics.

Kohl era ends with victory for Schröder

Defiant Blair tries to brush off Left's poll triumphs

A million on the move as hurricane gains strength

Carlton eyes Villa and Spurs

Oxford quest for its old sporting glory

The Times, *28 September, 98*

The answer is that they all have something to do with economics. It pervades so many areas of our lives. Economics is about making choices, and of course so is government. Many people would like a combination of low taxes on the one hand and high public expenditure on the other. Economics tells us that this is impossible. As the Nobel Prize-winning economist Milton Friedman said,

'There's no such thing as a free lunch.' Resources are limited, and if they are being used for one thing, the same resources, whether money, time or energy cannot be used for something else. Choices must be made.

For much of the twentieth century, there was an ideological divide over who would decide on the use of resources. Generally, the political Right favoured individuals and businesses being left free to decide for themselves how resources would be used. They therefore favoured low levels of tax and minimal interference by government in the running of the economy. On the other hand, the Left believed that a good proportion of resources should be controlled and used by government in order to provide things of benefit to society as a whole. The Left has therefore favoured higher taxes and higher levels of government spending.

Table 1: *Extracts from MORI polls and surveys for 1974–98 in Britain, showing the percentage results from two questions:*

1 What would you say is the most important issue facing Britain today?
2 What do you see as other important issues facing Britain today?

	UNEMPLOYMENT	NHS	LAW & ORDER	SCHOOLS/ EDUCATION	PRICES/ INFLATION	EU/ COMMON MARKET	ECONOMY ECONOMIC SITUATION
1974–82							
Sep '74	9	3	8	12	82	19	
Nov '77	50	10	n/a	12	64	n/a	
Aug '78	55	11	23	15	63	9	
Apr '79	53	17	41	17	68	14	
Apr '80	51	23	32	24	69	23	
Sep '82	87	n/a	13	n/a	32	4	
Sep '83	80	17	16	8	19	4	
Sep '84	70	10	10	7	21	5	
Sep '85	83	13	19	10	10	2	
Sep '86	78	19	17	11	7	1	
Sep '87	63	21	20	16	4	2	9
Sep '88	44	36	24	14	11	8	16
Sep '89	25	31	18	13	16	5	17
Sep '90	24	29	9	20	30	3	26
Sep '91	54	45	23	26	12	8	26
Aug '92	64	26	14	18	13	10	44
Sep '92	61	21	11	17	9	22	53
Sep '93	61	32	29	19	6	7	32
Sep '94	59	34	33	21	5	7	20
Sep '95	48	44	24	30	3	13	20
Sep '96	43	35	27	32	3	23	14
Sep '97	35	45	28	45	4	21	17
Sep '98	44	40	17	31	6	20	27

SOURCE: MORI (MARKET & OPINION RESEARCH INTERNATIONAL LTD)

Opinion polls constantly show that the public ranks 'economic' issues as the most important facing the country. Table 1 shows some of the results from two questions asked by MORI, one of Britain's leading market-research organisations. You can see that in September 1998, unemployment was considered the most important issue, with the NHS, education and the economy also receiving significant scores. These are all issues which people elect governments to deal with. If we were to go back in time, we would find that different issues dominated people's concerns. For example, in September 1974, MORI's poll saw inflation and prices as clearly the main issue facing the country, with a score of 82 per cent. The diagram below shows why that concern with prices may have evaporated.

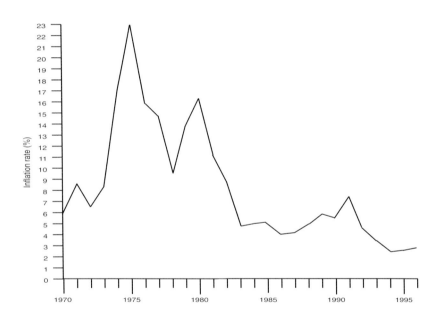

BRITISH INFLATION RATES (PERCENTAGE)

SOURCE: EUROSTAT

In what years do you think MORI would have found inflation to be mentioned as the most important issue facing Britian? This is a difficult question to answer, because we do not know what else was happening in those years. Very often in economics, a cure for one problem may result in a different problem, so it is small wonder that governments find it so difficult to manage the economy. In any case, the whole idea of managing the economy is a relatively new one, as we shall see.

This book will explain what economists mean by words like 'inflation', 'unemployment', 'balance of payments' and the other words concerning the economy that politicians have to deal with. It will describe how governments have tried to manage the economy since 1945, and will look at the economic policies of the three main parties. It will also examine the biggest economic issue facing Britain at the start of the new millennium, namely the European Union.

STUDY GUIDES

Practice Questions

The results of the *Times*–MORI political poll conducted over 18–21 September 1998 reveals:

- the lowest Economic Optimism Index (EOI) since October 1992
- the lowest Conservative share since November 1997
- Mr Hague's worst rating since –34 in November 1997
- that satisfaction with the government and Mr Blair is down
- the lowest net satisfaction with Mr Blair since February 1998.

1 Given this information, what would you expect to be people's answer to MORI's question: 'Do you think that the general economic condition of the country will improve, stay the same or get worse over the next 12 months?'?
2 What do you think that people now see as the most important economic issue facing the country? Why are economic issues so important?

2

GOVERNMENT CONTROL
OF THE ECONOMY

Introduction

THE IDEA THAT any government should have a role in the management of the economy is a very modern one in historical terms. As late as the 1930s, the rarely contested wisdom was that the government had no role in the economy except for the provision of public goods. In this chapter we will see how during the twentieth century, people have come to expect increasing levels of service from government, so that in Britain most people have health services, schools and pensions, all provided by the government in addition to the traditional government provision of law and order, and security. We will discover that in the second half of the century governments took on a very complex role in managing the economy, and that taxes were raised no longer simply to pay for government services, but also as a tool in economic management.

Key Points
- Public goods and merit goods.
- An increasing role for government.
- The 1930s: a new role for government.
- Demand and the circular flow of income.

PUBLIC GOODS AND MERIT GOODS

In the seventeenth century, the philosopher Thomas Hobbes wrote that without a strong central government, life would be 'nasty, brutish and short'. In those days, people expected very little from government, but they did expect one thing that only a strong government could give: security. Now we expect a lot more from government, but the 1980s and 1990s have seen a move in Britain for the government to provide less.

Even in a **free market economy**, there is a need for the government to produce some goods and services. This is because there is one category of goods and services which there is no incentive for a business to produce. These are called **public goods**. Think about the armed forces. If a private firm provided a navy and offered to use it to protect anyone who paid for the service, how would it work? Would you be any less protected by it if you didn't pay? The same is true of the police. It would be impractical for the police to only deter burglaries from houses that have bought the service, or only investigate murders of people who have paid for the murder investigation service.

The point is that there are some things which it would be impractical for private businesses to provide. Think about street lights. Once they are provided, you can't stop people who want to walk down the street benefiting from the lights whether or not they pay for them. Similarly, the fact that one person is benefiting from the light in no way diminishes the benefit available to someone else walking down the street.

Street lights, armed forces and the police are examples of public goods because they have two characteristics. They are:

1 non-excludable
2 indivisible.

Non-excludability simply means that once the good or (more likely) service is provided, it is not possible to stop people benefiting from it. 'Indivisibility' or 'non-rivalry' means that the fact that one person is benefiting from what is being provided does not reduce the benefit available to somebody else.

A good or service that has these two characteristics is called a 'public good' because it must be provided for the public by the government. It is not free because it still has to be paid for. One of the very basic roles of government is to provide the public goods of defence together with law and order. Government has the power of punishment, to ensure that people pay (through taxes) for public goods.

Many things provided by the government are not public goods, although they are free at the point of delivery and are paid for out of taxes. Schools are not public goods because clearly you can exclude non-payers from a school, as is the case with independent schools. Also, it is often argued that an extra person in the class does reduce the attention available to everyone else. Similarly, health is not a public good as people who cannot pay can be excluded (as in private hospitals), and one person having an operation clearly prevents other people from using the operating theatre at the same time. Therefore, both education and health fail the non-excludability and the indivisibility or non-rivalry tests.

In Britain, both education and health care are provided by the government for most people and paid for out of taxes. This is because governments have believed that people ought to have access to them. However, to what extent should people have their needs provided for by the government? We have noted that the USA does not have a National Health Service, but in Britain, should dental treatment be freely available to everyone?

Things that are paid for either wholly or partly by the government are called **merit goods**, and politicians disagree over what should be included as a merit good; for example, should dental treatment be a merit good? Merit goods need not necessarily be provided free at the time of use. Instead, the government could decide to encourage people to use something by making it cheaper than it otherwise would be. The government chooses to do this with some rail lines, giving the operator a **subsidy** to keep down fares and encourage people to use the service.

There are some things which the government wishes to discourage people from buying. It can either ban them (eg heroin) or make them more expensive than they otherwise would be by adding a tax (eg cigarettes). Goods which harmfully affect people when used are called **demerit goods**.

HOW ARE PUBLIC AND MERIT GOODS PAID FOR?

Although things such as health care and education may be free when you use them, they are not free to provide. They do have to be paid for, initially by the government; but the government gets its money mainly from taxes. Taxes can be divided into two types: direct and indirect. **Direct taxes** include **income tax**, **national insurance** and any other taxes that are charged directly on people's income or wealth. These taxes only apply to people earning above certain amounts. You may well not pay direct taxes but you will almost certainly pay **indirect taxes**. These are taxes on what you spend. The main one is **value-added tax (VAT)**. In 1999, VAT was charged at 17.5 per cent on everything you bought except: food, children's-size clothes, books, newspapers and public transport. (Gas and electricity were taxed at 5 per cent.) If you drive a car or motorbike, smoke tobacco or drink alcohol, you will be paying large additional taxes on these items, with leaded petrol being taxed more highly than unleaded. So, remember that even if you are not paying income tax, you are almost certainly a 'tax payer' and the next time the **Budget** is broadcast, it affects you!

---

1. The Chancellor's proposals will result in the following rates and bands for the tax year 1998–1999 (1997–1998 levels shown for comparison):

RATE OF TAX (PER CENT)	TAXABLE INCOME* 1997–1998 (POUNDS)	TAXABLE INCOME* 1998–1999 (POUNDS)
Lower (20)	0–4,100	0–4,300
Basic (23)	4,101–26,100	4,301–27,100
Higher (40)	over 26,100	over 27,100

*Taxable income is defined as gross income for tax purposes, less those allowances and reliefs available at the taxpayer's marginal rate.

---

2. The proposed levels of allowances for 1998–1998 are as follows (1997–1998 levels are shown for comparison):

ALLOWANCE	1997–1998 (POUNDS)	1998–1999 (POUNDS)
Personal allowance	4,045	4,195
Personal allowance (age 65–74)	5,220	5,410
Personal allowance (age 75 and over)	5,400	5,600
Married couple's allowance	1,830	1,900

SOURCE: HM TREASURY

Economists also describe taxes as proportional, progressive or regressive. A tax is **proportional** when the same percentage of tax is taken no matter how wealthy someone may be. A **progressive tax** is one where richer people pay a higher rate of tax than do poorer people. A **regressive tax** is one where poorer people pay a higher proportion of their income in tax than do richer people. A *flat-rate tax* (such as the Poll Tax of the late 1980s in Britain) is regressive because as your income rises, the proportion paid in tax falls.

AN INCREASING ROLE FOR GOVERNMENT

During the nineteenth and early twentieth centuries, there was general agreement that the government's only role in the economy was in the provision of public goods. Gradually, through the late nineteenth century, the need on the part of industry for a literate and numerate workforce led to elementary education becoming a merit good provided free of payment by the government.

The next extension in the role of government in the economy was led by David Lloyd George's and Prime Minister Herbert Asquith's Liberal government from 1906. The Budget Lloyd George submitted in 1909 contained numerous proposals for social legislation benefiting workers, and it met with vigorous opposition from the Conservatives and from the House of Lords, which voted it down. There followed a constitutional crisis when the Liberal government called a general election to obtain a **mandate** for the People's Budget to be passed into law. The government was returned with an overwhelming majority in the House of Commons, but this did not change the situation in the House of Lords which, with the exception of judges and bishops, was an entirely hereditary body with a huge Conservative majority. With the backing of the electorate, Prime Minister Asquith was able to present the House of Lords with an ultimatum: pass the Budget or the King would be asked to create 1,000 Liberal Lords who would vote the House of Lords out of existence. Faced with their imminent demise, the Lords passed the Budget, and shortly afterwards, the House of Lords was forbidden by law to consider finance bills, while many of Lloyd George's reforms were adopted, including national sickness and invalidity insurance and unemployment insurance.

Another way in which the Liberal government of the first decade of the twentieth century intervened in the market was in the field of pay. Although a national minimum wage was not enforced, a system was established whereby certain occupations were included in **wages councils**. Ironically, it was the hero of the Conservative Party, Winston Churchill, who championed the cause of these councils. He was at this time a member of the Liberal government, and support for the councils, where representatives of employers and employees met together to set national minimum wages in specific occupations, came from employers who were fearful that businesses handing out lower pay rates would produce goods at lower cost and sell their products more cheaply. Churchill argued that a bad employer could always be undercut by an even worse employer. The debate over wages councils rehearsed similar arguments to those of the late 1990s concerning, again, a national minimum wage, but wages councils themselves were to survive only until 1993.

By the 1930s, the government was beginning to intervene in the economy to provide a safety net in the form of public goods, education and some very limited welfare benefits. There was agreement within the political and economic mainstream that while the government should be able to provide some small benefit for the unemployed to stop them from starving, it should in no way interfere in the economy to try to reduce the level of unemployment.

THE 1930S: A NEW ROLE FOR GOVERNMENT

1929 saw the beginning of an economic **slump** throughout the industrialised world. Unemployment in Britain topped 3 million, amounting to over 20 per cent of the workforce. Across the USA and many European countries, the problem was even worse. However, while Conservative, Labour and National Unity governments were formed over the next few years to tackle the problem, they shared similar economic policies that forbade the government to intervene.

Some politicians did propose departures from the accepted models. The former Liberal Prime Minister Lloyd George called for a huge expansion in government spending on what we would now call the infrastructure, such as in road building. Oswald Moseley, the leader of the British Fascist movement, while still a Labour minister, argued for a combination of government spending and import controls. However, these were isolated voices.

The *Great Depression* of the 1930s bewildered economists and politicians alike. The economists continued to hold, against mounting evidence to the contrary, that time and nature would restore prosperity if the government refrained from manipulating the economy. Unfortunately, the generally accepted remedies (mainly cutting wages and government spending) simply did not work.

New explanations and fresh policies were urgently required, and this was what the economist John Maynard Keynes, departing from traditional or **neo-classical economics**, supplied. In his major work *The General Theory of Employment, Interest and Money* (1936), the central message translates into two powerful propositions. Existing explanations of unemployment he declared to be nonsense: neither high prices nor high wages could explain persistent depression and mass unemployment. Instead, he proposed an alternative explanation of these phenomena, focused on what he termed **aggregate demand**: that is, the total spending of consumers, business and government. When aggregate demand is low, sales and jobs suffer; when it is high, there is work for all. From this flowed a powerful and comprehensive view of economic behaviour that still forms the basis of contemporary **macroeconomics**. However, during the 1930s it was only people on the fringe of politics who supported his ideas. Meanwhile, in the USA, President Franklin Roosevelt's *New Deal* launched a massive programme of public works, while in Germany Adolf Hitler and the Nazis were engaged in a huge programme of military expenditure and building new autobahns which would facilitate the invasion of neighbouring countries.

Only as a response to the build-up of forces in Germany did the British government start to increase spending, but it proved Keynes's argument. It was only the increase in government spending in preparation for the Second World War that signalled an end to the Great Depression of the 1930s.

By the end of the Second World War in 1945, a new consensus had developed that the government had a duty to manage demand in the economy so that unemployment would be kept permanently low.

DEMAND AND THE CIRCULAR FLOW OF INCOME

The economic story of Britain since the Second World War has been described as **stop–go economics** or 'boom and bust'. Very simply, both Labour and Conservative governments have tried to achieve both low inflation and low unemployment. Inflation and unemployment are of course both unpopular, but the problem has been that whenever a government has tried to decrease unemployment, it has thereby increased the general level of demand in the economy, and this has led to inflation. On the other hand, attempts to reduce inflation have involved reducing demand, and this in turn has caused unemployment.

The 1980s began with a **recession** as the government tried to bring down inflation. Midway through the 1980s, the then Chancellor of the Exchequer, Nigel Lawson, thought that he had beaten inflation and so began to reduce interest rates so that people with mortgages and loans had more money to spend. The result was a fall in unemployment and a rise in inflation. Faced with an inflation rate in 1990 of near 10 per cent (higher than when the government came to office in 1979 with the control of inflation as its main target), interest rates were raised, and by 1993 the inflation rate was below 2 per cent but unemployment was now up to 10 per cent. This is what is meant by 'stop–go economics'.

THE MEANING OF AGGREGATE DEMAND

Aggregate demand comprises all the different demands for goods and services added together. Most of this demand comes from consumers, and this is called *consumption*, but firms also demand goods to help in the production process. This is called *investment*. The government is an important purchaser of goods and services, and so we must include *government spending*, and people living abroad may also demand things and so we also include the difference between exports and imports. Aggregate demand is thus C (consumption) + I (investment) + G (government spending) + (X – M) (exports minus imports), or C + I + G + (X – M).

THE CIRCULAR FLOW OF INCOME

The Circular Flow of Income gives a model of the economy. Economists use such models to draw a simplified picture of the way the economy works. By making them very simple, we can illustrate how certain things affect other things. A simple two-sector economy with no government and no foreign trade would

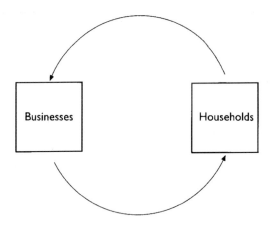

T<small>HE</small> C<small>IRCULAR</small> F<small>LOW OF</small> I<small>NCOME IN A</small> T<small>WO-SECTOR</small> E<small>CONOMY</small>

look as shown in the diagram above. In this model, for an economic system to exist, we must have households and firms. People live in households, and their role in the economy has two parts. First, according to this model, the *factors of production* (land, labour, capital and enterprise) are all owned by households. Firms hire these factors of production in exchange for a reward (*rent, wages, interest* and *profit* respectively). So, people live in households, and earn money from firms by hiring to firms something that the households have and the firms need. For most households, this will be labour – the ability to work. Since most households can offer this, the reward (wages) will not be very high unless there is something special about the labour (a high level of skill, a willingness to do dangerous or unpleasant work, or a high level of qualification). On the other hand, the owners of the land, capital and enterprise are much more scarce, and so these people can become very rich. Their services are in relatively short supply.

Households earn their money from firms, and so there is a flow of income from firms to households. But from where do firms get their money to pay the households? Well, the second job of households is to buy up the output of firms (consumption), and so there is also a flow of income from households to firms. Firms rely on households for their income just as households rely on firms.

Note that in this very simply model, households must spend all of their income on the output of firms. There is nothing else they can do with it because we have not given them the option of *saving*. This is clearly an unrealistic scenario, and so we can make our model a little nearer the real world by adding a financial or banking sector where households can save. But what do banks do with this money that is saved with them? They lend it out in return for interest. Firms now have access to income in addition to that which comes from households directly, and this is called investment. (See the diagram on page 13.)

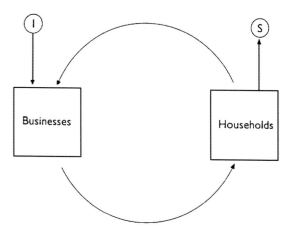

THE CIRCULAR FLOW OF INCOME WITH SAVING AND INVESTMENT ADDED

Before a financial sector was introduced into the model, the economy was always in balance or **equilibrium** because the income flowing to both households and firms was always equal. Households had to spend all of their income on the output of firms because there was nothing else they could do with it. Now, rather than spend all of their income, they can choose to save some instead. Any such income that is saved will not then be spent on goods and services produced by firms, and so firms will now have less income to pay for the hire of the factors of production. However, firms now also have the option of borrowing for investment. The banks will want people to save with them so that they can use that money to lend to people at high rates of interest.

Now, note that if firms borrow for investment more than households save (which can be done in the short term), then, overall the amount of money flowing around the circular flow will increase. However, if firms invest less than people save, then the money in the circular flow will decrease. And if (and this is most unlikely) saving = investment, the economy is in equilibrium.

Injection0 and withdrawal0

We now have an opportunity for extra money to enter the circular flow of income in the form of investment. Similarly, money can leave the circular flow through savings. Any money entering the circular flow is called an **injection**, while money leaving is known as a **leakage** or a *withdrawal*. In a real economy, savings and investment (comprising the financial sector) are not the only ways in which income can enter or leave the circular flow. There are two other sectors: the government and foreign trade.

When people are taxed, their spending power is reduced. Therefore, not all of their income will return to firms: some of their income will go to the government instead. So, taxation is a withdrawal. However, the government then spends the money, and such government spending is an injection.

Much of what we buy is not made by firms in our own country. The money to pay for these imports goes to firms abroad who use it to pay the factors of production in their own economy. So, although goods are coming into this country, money is thus also flowing out, and so imports are a withdrawal. Similarly, when foreigners buy goods from this country, the money to pay for these exports flows *into* our firms, and so exports are an injection. (See the diagram below.)

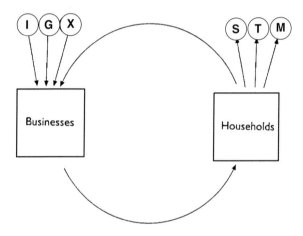

THE CIRCULAR FLOW OF INCOME WITH ALL INJECTIONS AND LEAKAGES ADDED

The economy is in equilibrium when all injections added together are equal to all withdrawals added together.

The multiplier effect

Remember, the circular flow of income means that when any money is in the system, it will flow between households and firms until it gradually disappears through leakages. This means that any extra money injected into the circular flow will also flow between households and firms until it disappears through leakages. Just how quickly it disappears will be determined by the size of the leakages. If people save a big proportion of their income, the amount passed on through extra consumption will be less than if people spend all of it. So, any injection into the circular flow of income will increase spending not by the original size of the injection but by several times the size of the injection. This is called the **multiplier effect** because any injection is multiplied.

The county of Cornwall does not have a university. Suppose the government decided to create a new university on a greenfield site on the edge of Truro. (The construction industry is very dependent on government spending, and spending money on a new construction project is a good way of ensuring a high multiplier effect because very little of the spending goes on imports.) Consider how this decision would affect the local economy. First of all, the university would be built. This would create jobs for construction workers. These workers will spend their money in local shops and businesses, and the owners of these shops and businesses will in turn then have more money to spend. After the building is complete, people will be employed in the university doing all sorts of jobs. Many of these people will be lecturers, and they are paid above the national average. Then they will move to the area, creating extra demand for houses (pulling up prices and possibly leading to new houses being built) and spending money in shops and local businesses. The initial increase in spending by the government will thus be passed on, raising the spending levels of many individuals who are not being paid directly by the government. This multiplier effect takes place whenever there is an injection into the circular flow of income.

FISCAL AND MONETARY POLICY

This chapter has concentrated on aggregate demand only, but an increase in demand without an accompanying increase in *supply* will lead to higher prices. Very simply, when demand for a given good rises but firms are unable to increase supply, the price goes up to ration who gets the limited supply of the good. Similarly, if aggregate demand increases and the country's ability to supply the goods and services demanded cannot keep up, then average prices will rise, and this is **inflation**.

It is a relatively simple task for the government to control inflation: it can simply reduce aggregate demand by using either **fiscal** or **monetary policy**. Fiscal policy uses taxes and government spending to regulate the economy at the time of the Budget. To reduce aggregate demand, taxes can be raised or government spending can be reduced. If the aim is to stop prices from rising, then it would not be advisable to raise taxes on spending, such as VAT, so it is generally income tax that is raised. Increasing taxes or cutting government expenditure on major items is politically unpopular. Monetary policy involves the Bank of England's adjusting **interest rates**. If interest rates go up, then people will borrow less and save more. This will leave less money available for consumption and investment. This too is politically unpopular as it makes people worse off; indeed, some people will be unable to keep up their mortgage repayments, and some businesses will be unable to repay their bank loans.

The problem with both these policies is that by reducing the demand for goods and services, they have the knock-on effect of reducing the need for workers. The demand for labour is known as a *derived demand* because it is based on (or, more technically, derived from) the demand for goods and services. So, reducing aggregate demand leads to unemployment. If reducing unemployment is a priority, then policies to increase aggregate demand will be used. Fiscal policy can be used by cutting taxes or increasing government expenditure, and monetary policy can be used by reducing interest rates, making it easier to borrow and less attractive to save.

SUMMARY

In this chapter, we have seen how the government has gradually become involved in the management of the economy. In the years immediately following the Second World War, both Conservative and Labour governments considered it their duty to manage aggregate demand so that unemployment was kept low. They achieved this by following the principles of Keynes. We will go on in later chapters to consider how this consensus broke down in the 1970s and look at the policies on unemployment of today's politicians.

However, in this chapter we have established the basic principles of economic management. Aggregate demand comprises consumption (spending by households), investment (spending by businesses), government spending and the difference between exports and imports. An increase in any of these areas will create a multiplier effect whereby the original increase in demand carries on increasing spending by some multiple of the original increase.

The government can use fiscal policy to regulate aggregate demand. This is done at the time of the Budget, and it involves using government spending and taxes to either increase or decrease the level of spending in the economy.

On a monthly basis, the Monetary Committee of the Bank of England sets interest rates to regulate the amount of spending in the economy. This is called monetary policy.

Activities

1 Decide whether each of the following is a public or a merit good:
   a the Police
   b the Navy
   c the National Health Service
   d Clacton County High School
   e Chelmsford College of Further Education
   f the Fire Brigade
   g the University of Brighton.

For answers to this question, see p 117 at the back of the book.

2 (Research)
  a What is the current base rate of income tax?
  b What is the current rate of national insurance?
  c How much can somebody earn before they start paying income tax?
  d Somebody earns £18,000 a year. Some of that is tax free. The rest will be taxed at the base rate. National insurance is paid on all of it. How much tax is paid, and how much is left of the £18,000?

3 Draw a circular flow diagram with just households and firms. Now for each of the following situations, write the appropriate letter on the diagram, with an arrow indicating whether it is an injection or a leakage.
  a a family depositing money into a building society account
  b the building of a new hospital by the National Health Service
  c a business borrowing £3 million from a bank to build a new factory
  d a family buying a BMW car made in Germany
  e the purchase of concert tickets in London by a group of American tourists.

STUDY GUIDES

Revision Hints

This chapter has given background information on the government's involvement in the economy. Your note-taking should concentrate on the following:

• the characteristics of public and merit goods
• the differences between direct and indirect tax
• the way in which Keynes's views differed from traditional views of government and the economy
• how governments can manage aggregate demand
• the difference between fiscal and monetary policy.

Exam Hints

While the information contained may not directly answer questions set in your A-level paper, you need to understand why governments intervened to manage the economy after the Second World War, and understand that there was a consensus between political parties on the general direction of economic policy for most of this century. Time has been much more important than ideology in determining government economic policy. This may seem surprising when differences over the economy play such an important part in elections, but we will see that differences between parties have been differences of emphasis only with all parties, in fact, subscribing to the economic orthodoxy of a given time.

Practice Questions

1 What effect did the economist John Maynard Keynes have on British politics in the period after 1945?

2 'The public always wants more from their government.' Why may they be unable to have it?

3

WHEN SHOULD GOVERNMENTS INTERVENE?

Introduction

SINCE 1979, THE Conservative government in Britain had attempted to move as much business activity as possible from the public sector to the private sector. They believed that 'markets work'. Sixteen years later, however, there were still activities that had to be carried on by the government. We saw in Chapter 2 that in any country, the government will have to provide 'public goods', and that just what else the government is involved in is a political choice. It is also the case that without government regulation, monopolies can exploit consumers, and there would be no restrictions on pollution, for example.

It is true that in the late 1990s the government in Britain intervenes in the economy far less than it did in the 1970s, but there are still many ways in which the government affects prices, incomes and the goods and services that can be produced.

In this chapter we will see that there are a number of ways in which the government (a term describing not only central government in London but also local governments, ie city, district, borough and county councils, and the European Union) intervenes in economic activity to try to bring about desired ends. These interventions may be to encourage people to buy something (as in the case of mortgages for buying a house) or they may encourage greater production (as in the case of guaranteed prices for farmers through the Common Agricultural Policy, CAP). Similarly, the government may use taxes to discourage the consumption of cigarettes, or to encourage people to switch from leaded to unleaded petrol.

Key Points

- The meaning of positive and normative economics.
- The Common Agricultural Policy.
- The market for homes.
- Other subsidies.
- Indirect taxes.

THE MEANING OF POSITIVE AND NORMATIVE ECONOMICS

The title of this chapter asks a question that includes the word 'should'. This is not a question that an economist can answer as an economist. The word 'should' implies some moral judgement. Economics can point to the consequences and effects of such judgements, but it is then up to individuals who are armed with the information and understanding gained from reading this book to answer the political question: 'When should governments intervene in markets?'

If we make the statement 'Governments intervene in markets', we can show that this is true. Such a statement is known as a *positive* statement. However, if we introduce the word 'should' and say 'Governments should intervene in markets', we have changed the statement to one which is *normative*, which is for politicians rather than economists. However, it is important to remember that well-known economists do also of course have political points of view. The most famous and influential economist of the twentieth century, John Maynard Keynes, was a member of the Liberal Party, and his starting point for the invention of the concept of aggregate demand and of the structure of macroeconomics (see from Chapter 2 onwards) was that he passionately believed unemployment to be a bad thing.

This is why economists disagree. Depending on their political view of the world, they will make different assumptions about how people behave and about the relative importance of different economic problems. At a very simple level, rightwing economists believe that the best way to reduce unemployment is to reduce pay so that workers become more affordable for firms. On the other hand, leftwing economists believe that the best way to reduce unemployment is for the government to spend more both on training and on projects such as new schools and hospitals that will require extra people to work. Both sides can pick out economic theory, and indeed real-world statistics, to prove their point.

THE COMMON AGRICULTURAL POLICY

Perhaps the main way in which most of us are affected by government intervention in the economy is through the **Common Agricultural Policy**, because this makes our food more expensive than it otherwise would be. The CAP was developed because after the Second World War, European governments were worried that Western Europe was relying too heavily on food imports. During the war, both sides had suffered from food shortages, and cheap food supplies had to be shipped in from overseas.

The founding countries of the European Economic Community (now the European Union (EU) – see Chapter 8) decided that they needed a system to encourage farmers first to stay in agriculture (rather than continue the historic trend of taking better jobs in towns) and second to increase production. All the members of the EU agree that the central authority in Brussels can run this Common Agricultural Policy, which works as follows. Each year, a guaranteed minimum price is set for a range of farm products, eg beef, olive oil, wine, apples or butter. If the market equilibrium price lies above that minimum price, then the market operates in the normal way. However, in the many countries, such as France and Germany, where farmers can play an important role at elections, politicians are under pressure to raise the minimum guaranteed price each year so that it lies above the equilibrium price. At this higher-than-equilibrium price, consumers demand a smaller quantity while producers supply a greater quantity. In a free market, the price would fall to the equilibrium and the producers would cut back production. However, the point of the CAP was to encourage farmers to increase production by guaranteeing them a price that made it worthwhile for them to produce more. The EU, therefore, steps in and buys up any excess production that results from the high price so that farmers do not cut their price to sell off stock. (See the diagram below.)

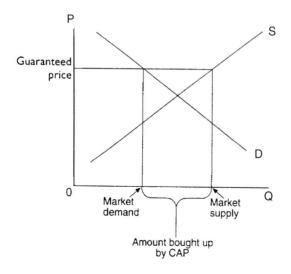

THE CAP AND THE GUARANTEED PRICE

In the past, the EU has bought huge amounts of excess agricultural products. The name given to this process is *intervention buying*. In theory, the products are stored and could be introduced back into the market if there were a particularly bad harvest one year, so that prices would be kept stable. In reality, this has never happened. Therefore, these great surpluses have become known as the 'wine lake' and the 'butter mountain'.

In the 1990s, the policy has been modified to introduce *quotas*. Here, a minimum price is still guaranteed, but a farmer is only allowed to produce up to a certain quantity. They are allocated a 'quota'. If a farmer produces more milk than their quota permits, they must pour it down the drain or find some other use for it.

The result of the CAP is that producers have a guaranteed income each year. Farmers often complain that this income is not enough, but there are very few businesses that have a guaranteed income. Consumers pay for this in two ways, first by being charged more than the equilibrium price, and second through taxes being used both to buy up the extra supply and to pay for the storage.

In the 1990s, there have been attempts to cut the oversupply of certain products by encouraging farmers to stop producing so much. 'Set-aside' is a scheme where farmers are paid money not to grow crops on some of their land. There are also payments (subsidies) for uprooting apple orchards so that fewer apples are produced. These are all ways of trying to affect the quantity produced without letting prices fall.

THE MARKET FOR HOMES

For some years, Britain has had a problem where there are not enough homes for people who need somewhere to live. For most of the twentieth century, local councils have had the responsibility of housing people who cannot buy their own house. The Conservative government from 1979 onwards believed that housing should be in the private rather than the public sector.

There are few people who are able to rent out a property for someone else to live in. This means that property to rent is in short supply but in great demand. This leads to very high prices being charged. Is it right, therefore, to introduce 'rent controls', making rents cheaper than they otherwise would be? The rent control reduces the rent to below the equilibrium price (see the diagram on page 23). This makes properties more affordable. At the same time, landlords find that because they will get less rent, it is less worthwhile supplying property. So the effect of a rent control is that more people who can afford the rents charged but fewer places are available to rent. (Does this make the problem better or worse? What do you think?)

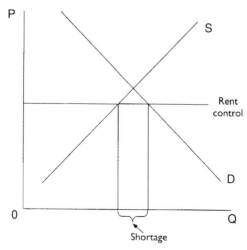

RENT CONTROL AND THE EQUILIBRIUM PRICE

Also, from 1979, people have been encouraged to buy their own home rather than to rent. In European terms, this is a British obsession. In Britain it has become quite normal for people to take out a mortgage and eventually own their own house. In other countries (eg Germany) this is quite rare. To encourage people to buy their own home, there was a policy for many years (extending back to well before 1979) that people received help from the government. The mortgage repayments were considered to be something desirable, a sort of merit good. Governments decided that the part of people's income which they used to pay the interest on their mortgage should not be taxed. People could claim back the tax, so that their mortgage repayments were effectively subsidised by the government. Since the 1980s, this subsidy has gradually been reduced, and by the time you read this book, it may have disappeared.

Why has a government, whose political aim was to encourage people to buy their own home, withdrawn a subsidy to help them to do this? Look at the diagram on page 24. As a result of Mortgage Interest Tax Relief (MIRAS) or a mortgage subsidy, buyers of houses can afford to pay more for houses. However, the supply of houses is relatively fixed (ie there is limited scope for building more houses). The effect of the subsidy is to increase the price of houses, but it does not encourage many extra houses to be supplied because most houses are bought from people who are looking to move to another house.

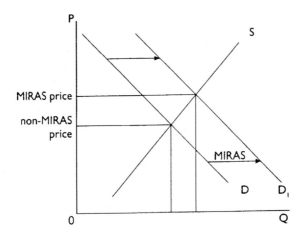

THE EFFECT OF MIRAS ON THE PRICE OF HOUSES

OTHER SUBSIDIES

From time to time, various goods have been subsidised to make them cheaper than they otherwise would be. Mortgage Interest Tax Relief is an example of a subsidy to the consumer which results in the price going up. In the late 1970s, basic foods such as bread were subsidised. In this case, the subsidy was given to the producer to make the product cheaper than it otherwise would be.

A producer subsidy shifts the supply curve to the right, causing the price to fall and the quantity bought to increase – see the diagram below.

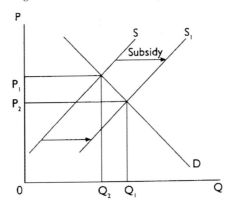

THE EFFECT OF SUBSIDIES TO PRODUCERS ON THE PRICE AND THE QUANTITY DEMAND OF A GOOD

INDIRECT TAXES

Indirect taxes, as we saw, are taxes on spending. In addition to being an important source of tax revenue for the government, they can be used to influence consumer behaviour. Food, children's-size clothes, books, newspapers and public transport are all zero rated for value-added tax (VAT). In other words, the government takes the view that people should be encouraged to buy these items. Other goods and services have VAT charged on them at 17.5 per cent (correct in 1999). So, the government can decide to take tax off things where it wants to encourage consumption. Other things it can make *more* expensive in order to *discourage* consumption. Cigarettes are the obvious example, where most of the price of a packet of cigarettes goes as tax to the government. There is an economic argument for this in that smokers cost the country more. They are much more likely to be off work sick than are non-smokers, they are likely to need more medical treatment for long terminal illnesses, and they make non-smokers buy more washing liquid to get the smell of smoke out of their clothes.

The switch to unleaded petrol by most cars in the late 1980s began when the then Chancellor of the Exchequer made the tax on leaded petrol higher than that for unleaded. This is one of the best examples of the government using the tax system to influence consumer behaviour.

The diagram below shows that an indirect tax shifts the supply curve to the left, making the price higher and reducing the quantity consumed. Of course, the effect of the tax will depend on the **elasticity of demand** for the product. This simply means that it will depend on what alternatives are available. Unleaded petrol provided a close substitute for leaded, but there are no obvious close substitutes for nicotine.

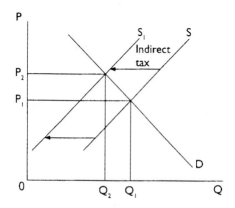

THE EFFECT OF AN INDIRECT TAX ON THE PRICE AND THE QUANTITY DEMANDED OF A GOOD

The Government recognises that, for many people especially in isolated areas, car ownership is not a choice but a necessity and so I now want to re-balance car taxation so that it falls less on car ownership. And I want to make the change in an environmentally sensitive way.

From January next year, I am cutting the licence fee for lorries and buses with clean engines by up to £500. But I also want a major reform of the licence fee for cars. From next year I plan to reduce the fee for cars with the lowest emissions. From the cleanest and smallest cars, I plan to cut the licence fee by £50.

And, as we make the preparations for this long term environmental change, for this year I propose, at a cost of £145 million, to freeze the licence fee for all vehicles. To encourage lower emissions, the costs of converting company cars to road fuel gases will, from now, be disregarded for income tax purposes. At the same time I am increasing the scale charges for fuel provided by an employer, which will cost the typical company car user around £1 a week. The duty on road fuel gases will be frozen, increasing the incentive to use these cleaner fuels.

The last Government introduced a road fuel escalator, the principle of which we supported. They set it at 5 per cent. Since July it has been 6 per cent. There is agreement that only with the use of an escalator can emission levels be reduced by 2010 towards our commitments.

Gordon Brown, Chancellor of the Exchequer, from his 1998 Budget Speech.

RECENT POLICY

HM Customs and Excise 17

17 March 1998

FUEL DUTIES INCREASED TO IMPROVE URBAN AIR QUALITY AND REDUCE GREENHOUSE GAS EMISSIONS

The Chancellor has announced that from 6 pm tonight the tax (duty plus VAT) on road fuels will increase in line with the Government's commitment to raise road fuel duties by at least 6 per cent a year above inflation. The increases in this Budget will discourage unnecessary journeys and encourage fuel efficient vehicles. They are expected to produce carbon savings of about one million tonnes per year by 2001. Additionally, bringing forward the escalator increases to March each year should produce further carbon savings of 0.7 million tonnes per year.

The Chancellor also announced today his intention to change the structure of taxes on road fuels over time to improve the quality of air in urban areas, through two broad objectives:

- to tax petrol and diesel more fairly, based on the energy and carbon content. This means that the tax on a litre of diesel should be higher than that on petrol.
- to encourage all users of diesel to switch to ultra low sulphur diesel, a significantly cleaner fuel.

As a first step to achieving these objectives, the tax (duty plus VAT) on leaded and unleaded petrol will rise by 4.9p a litre and 4.4p a litre respectively. Ordinary diesel will go up by 5.5p a litre. The difference in duty between leaded and super-unleaded petrol has been cut from 1.5p a litre of 0.5p a litre and the duty on leaded petrol has been increased by almost 0.5p a litre more than that on unleaded.

The difference in duty between diesel and ultra low sulphur diesel is being increased from 1p to 2p. At the same time, the specification of ultra low sulphur diesel is being tightened to ensure that this fuel continues to offer significant improvements in urban air quality.

The duty on road fuel gases – which offer environmental benefits over petrol and diesel – is frozen again. This move complements the change to the company car tax regime to ignore the cost of conversion to gas and will further encourage gas powered vehicles.

HM Treasury.

SUMMARY

- Governments intervene in markets to regulate monopolies.
- Governments intervene in markets to limit pollution.
- Governments intervene in markets to encourage the consumption of socially desirable (merit) goods and services.
- Governments intervene in markets to discourage the use of socially undesirable (demerit) goods and services.
- Governments intervene using the following methods which have these effects:

INTERVENTION METHOD	EFFECT ON PRICE	EFFECT ON QUANTITY BOUGHT
Guaranteed minimum price	Increase	Decrease
Consumer subsidy	Increase	Increase
Producer subsidy	Decrease	Increase
Indirect tax	Increase	Decrease

Revision Hints

You need to have a set of notes that will help you to understand how governments have intervened in the economy to achieve specific policy objectives such as increased home ownership (through MIRAS). You will also need to know how governments can affect behaviour through subsidies and through the use of taxes. Nigel Lawson's introduction of different tax bands for leaded and unleaded petrol is the classic example here. Do not worry too much about learning the diagrams as these will not be required in the exam. They are used here simply to illustrate the point.

Exam Hints

Government actions in the economy can change quickly. It is quite possible that by the time you read this book, MIRAS will have been totally abolished. Therefore, you must be able to report the up-to-date position. The Treasury has a very useful web site that can be of assistance here. Its address is: http://www.hm-treasury.gov.uk.

Understanding the process by which taxes affect people's behaviour is the most important consideration. Tax makes a product more expensive and therefore reduces consumers' demand for the product. Alternatively, a subsidy will make things cheaper and therefore encourage people to buy them.

Practice Questions

1 Why is the government committed to increasing fuel duty by at least 6 per cent above the rate of inflation each year? How can changes in tax affect the environment?

2 Why does the government grant tax relief on mortgage repayments? Suggest why governments of both parties have been willing to greatly reduce the level of MIRAS.

4

PRIVATISATION

Introduction

FROM 1945 UNTIL 1979, many British industries were transferred from ownership by individuals in the private sector to ownership by government in the public sector. Public-sector businesses, ie *nationalised industries*, are under the control of the relevant cabinet minister in the government. For example, the National Health Service is a nationalised industry, and the Secretary of State for Health is ultimately responsible for it. The Post Office is part of the Secretary of State for Trade and Industry's responsibilities.

In this chapter we will see that the policy of privatisation developed over a number of years and took various forms. Each privatisation was opposed by the Labour Party, but in government, New Labour has not only abandoned any plans for renationalisation but is itself looking to more privatisation as a means of raising revenue. We will see that in many cases, privatisation (or more strictly denationalisation) has transferred monopolies from the public sector to the private sector where the free market would encourage them to work against the interest of consumers. A regulatory system has therefore been put in place to control these monopolies.

Key Points
- The reasons for nationalisation.
- The meaning of privatisation.
- Why privatise?
- Party privatisation policies, as at the 1997 General Election.

THE REASONS FOR NATIONALISATION

Unions have challenged Trade and Industry Secretary Peter Mandelson to keep the faith and not privatise the Post Office.

Derek Hodgson, general secretary of the Communication Workers' Union, attacked party spin doctors and rumours that the government was looking at selling off the service.

His speech received a rousing standing ovation from areas of the hall in marked contrast to the seated applause Mr Mandelson received.

The exchange repeated scenes at the TUC conference two weeks ago where Mr Mandelson was urged to calm union fears on privatisation plans.

Mr Hodgson said: 'No more speculation, no more spin, no decay, carry out the policy, keep the faith with those who have loyally supported you and tell us the Post Office is not going to be privatised or broken up with shares.'

Mr Hodgson condemned rumours which wanted to destroy the 'proud public service industry' by privatisation or priority share sales.

BBC/Labour Party Conference October 1998

Although the policy of **nationalisation** was largely associated with Labour governments, Conservative governments from 1951 to 1964 and from 1970 to 1974 not only accepted the existence of most nationalised industries but actually carried out nationalisation themselves, as in the case of British Leyland and Rolls Royce.

Reasons for nationalisation were varied, but included the following:

- *Reducing costs:* it was thought that bringing together lots of small companies into one large enterprise would reduce costs through the benefits of **economies of scale**. (These are savings that occur as a result of the increased size of a business; for example, the ability to buy in bulk or to put more resources into research and development.) The coal industry comprised a series of independent mines throughout the country until the 1940s, and no one mine had the money for major investment.
- *Improved management*: when the great names of the railway industry, such as the Great Western and the LNER, disappeared in 1947 to create British Rail (BR), these companies were on their last legs. Although the railway companies were regional monopolies, they were regarded as poorly managed. The government could now recruit the best managers and put them in charge of a national network. The problem, however, was that the government never paid British Rail management enough to attract the best managers.

- *Control of monopolies*: the gas industry, electricity industry, railway industry, water industry and telecommunications industry all share two characteristics: they have been run in the public sector and they are monopolies. Many people believe that where it is impractical to have competition in an industry, the government should own this industry, set its prices and spend any of its profits for the public good.
- *Political reasons*: the 1945 Labour government was committed to nationalising the coal industry because it was believed that the safety and well being of coal miners was being sacrificed to make private profit. The National Union of Mineworkers believed that the government would take better care of miners than did private companies. The government was also able to set social objectives for industries such as electricity where it chose to make electricity cheaper than a profit-making private-sector company would.
- *Saving businesses*: Rolls Royce is an example of a company which had gone bankrupt in the 1970s but which the Conservative government of Edward Heath did not want to disappear. Relatively few jobs were at stake, but the name of Rolls Royce was a source of British pride which had to be saved. On the other hand, the threatened closure of British Leyland, the only British mass producer of British cars, threatened not only prestige but also many thousands of jobs. (British Leyland changed its name to The Rover Group. It was sold in 1988 to British Aerospace who in turn sold it to the German care manufacturer BMW in 1994. So, there are now no British-owned mass car manufacturers.)

In 1979, Margaret Thatcher became Prime Minister, and her Conservative government adopted a policy of transferring nationalised industries from the public to the private sector. This process is part of **privatisation**, but strictly speaking it is **denationlisation**: privatisation describes something much broader.

THE MEANING OF PRIVATISATION

Privatisation describes the process of shifting the balance in the provision of services from the public to the private sector. In addition to the complete denationalisation of industries, it has taken the following forms:

- *the sale of public-sector property*. Most noticeably, local councils have been forced to sell council houses to the people who live in them. The longer that someone has lived in a council house, the cheaper it becomes for them to buy it. When the house is sold, the council receives the purchase price, but this is insufficient to build new property. In any case, central government has prevented local councils from spending this money, so the number of council houses has decreased.
- *compulsory competitive tendering*. This means that contracts for services which have traditionally been provided by local councils, such as rubbish collection, now

have to be awarded to the private firm that offers to provide the service at the lowest price. Often, a private company will employ the people who used to work for the council, and in many instances it is the council's own workforce that has won the contract. For example, in Colchester, local services are provided by Colchester Contract Services, a business owned by Colchester Borough Council. Cleaning and catering in hospitals and schools has also been 'put out to tender', and the question is often asked 'Is cheapest best?' It can be argued that standards of cleanliness and nutrition have fallen as a result of tendering.

- *sale of part of a nationalised industry.* Sometimes, parts of industries are seen as attractive to the private sector. For example, Sealink Ferries was originally part of British Rail. By 1984, the government was not ready to denationalise British Rail. That would have to wait for another decade. However, it did separate Sealink from British Rail and then sell it.
- *deregulation.* This means the relaxing of rules governing who can do what. One of the best-known examples of deregulation is in bus routes where until the early 1980s certain bus companies were licensed to operate certain routes. This prevented competition, and so, it was argued, kept fares high and service poor. Over the last decade, bus companies have had more freedom to operate where they choose. However, it can be argued that this has led to bus companies' concentrating on racing with each other to provide services on popular routes while people living in less populated areas have seen their bus service decrease or disappear. This process is sometimes called 'cherry picking', and it has implications for the privatisation of British Rail.

Table 2: *Major sales of public-sector businesses to the private sector*	
1979	British Petroleum (only partly state owned)
1981	British Aerospace Cable and Wireless Amersham International
1982	National Freight Corporation Britoil
1983	British Rail Hotels (part of BR)
1984	Sealink Ferries (part of BR) Jaguar Cars (part of British Leyland) British Telecom
1986	British Gas
1987	British Airways Rolls Royce Leyland Bus (part of British Leyland) Leyland Trucks (part of British Leyland) Royal Ordinance British Airports Authority

1988	British Steel
	British Leyland (sold to British Aerospace)
1989	British Water Authorities
1990	Electricity Boards
1991	Electricity Generation
1995	British Coal
1996	British Rail

WHY PRIVATISE?

The privatisation programme of the Conservative government has had several objectives:

REDUCING COSTS

Nationalised industries were seen as inefficient. They made large losses that then had to be paid for out of taxes. This encouraged workers to be lazy, and there was overmanning as there was no incentive for managers to produce at a low cost. On the other hand, private-sector managers have every incentive to produce at as low a cost as possible, otherwise they will lose their jobs.

The problem was that nationalised industries did make large losses. This was often because the government told them to. As **monopoly** suppliers, they could charge what they liked, but in the 1970s they were told to adopt **marginal cost pricing**, in other words charge a price that was equal to the extra cost of providing the service to that customer, rather than a higher price to cover average costs. Nationalised industries proved that they could easily make profits by putting their prices up before denationalisation and making large profits so that they were attractive to potential buyers.

CLAUSE FOUR DEFIANCE IS INFANTILE, SAYS BLAIR

By Robert Shrimsley in Brussels and George Jones

Mr Tony Blair has delivered a stinging rebuke to Labour Euro-MPs who defied his plans to rewrite the party's Clause Four – a commitment to wholesale nationalisation.

At a private meeting in Brussels, he accused them of 'gross discourtesy' and 'infantile incompetence' which had blunted his New Year political offensive.

Mr Blair left them in no doubt of his anger and frustration over the way their placing of a newspaper advertisement challenging his effort to update Clause Four had wrecked his first visit to Brussels as Labour leader.

The tensions within the party over the issue were demonstrated when Mr Blair was heckled and jeered by a handful of hard-Left MEPs. A furious Mr Blair told them to 'grow up' and stop indulging in the 'gesture politics' which could cost Labour the next election.

'Bambi' no more

Although his dressing-down for the MEPs had been widely expected, the strength of his criticism caused surprise at Westminster. The Labour leader has been nicknamed 'Bambi' and derided by Tory MPs for being bland. He seized the chance yesterday to demonstrate that there was a tough politician behind the 'nice guy' image.

His outburst has raised the stakes in his attempts to replace Clause Four with a modern statement of Labour's principles and values. Labour MPs spoke last night of growing concern among activists and trade unionists over the abandonment of what they saw as the core commitment to nationalisation and common ownership.

A Labour front-bencher said there was a feeling that Mr Blair had sought to 'bounce' the party into making the change.

The Daily Telegraph, *12 January 1995*

INCREASING CHOICE AND ENCOURAGING INNOVATION

Public-sector businesses have no incentive to innovate, that is to come up with new ideas. In the private sector, firms are continually trying to develop new ideas to beat the competition. It is certainly true that when British Telecom started to face competition in the supply of telephone equipment, new designs emerged, and the country quickly switched from the slow-dial to the push-button 'phone. However, this was a result of British Telecom's losing its monopoly on the supply of equipment rather than of the change in ownership of BT. When ITV started in the 1950s and 1960s, the BBC reacted to the competition by significantly increasing the quality of its programmes. The BBC was able to do this while remaining in the public sector. Many people are now worried that the proliferation of television channels will actually reduce the choice of good-quality programmes since, for companies faced with small market shares, it will not be worthwhile to produce good-quality television.

IMPROVING QUALITY

In the public sector, if customers are dissatisfied with the service they receive, they can complain, but there is no incentive for the provider of the service to improve things. In the private sector, a business that fails to please its customers will go out of business. In the 1990s, the government introduced the 'Citizens' Charter' which set out minimum standards of service that could be expected from businesses in the public sector. For example, if your train was more than an hour late, you would receive some compensation.

ECONOMIC FREEDOM

In 1995, Michael Heseltine proposed the denationalisation of Royal Mail. However, he was unable to go ahead because he found that several Conservative MPs thought that this would be 'a privatisation too far!'. The Trade Secretary's argument was that, as a private company, Royal Mail would be able to borrow money for investment and get involved in a wider range of business activities. However, many MPs argued that it was only the government's own rules that stopped Royal Mail from doing those things now.

WIDER SHARE OWNERSHIP

A major goal of the Conservative government has been to increase the number of people owning shares. In their own words, they have sought to create 'a share-owning democracy'. Certain denationalisations have involved heavy promotion of small allocations of shares to members of the public. Gas and electricity shares could be bought for relatively small amounts. Some of the thinking was that workers who own shares would see themselves as capitalists rather than just workers. Workers may then be more interested in making profits rather than in concentrating on pay increases. However, most denationalisations have simply involved the government selling the public-sector business to an existing private-sector business. Even where members of the public have been encouraged to buy shares, within a year many shares have been bought up by financial institutions. Since the policy of privatisation began, the proportion of the population that owns shares is only a little higher than it ever was before.

RAISING REVENUE

One important consequence of denationalising a business, particularly very large ones like gas, electricity or water (all examples of *utilities*), is that it raises billions of pounds for the government. This has allowed the government to charge rates of tax that are lower then they otherwise would be. The former Conservative Prime Minister Harold Macmillan, speaking as Lord Stockton a few years before his death in 1986, pointed to a problem with this policy. He described it as 'selling the family silver'. In other words, selling a valuable asset raises lots of money in the short term, but once it's sold, it cannot be sold again, and the problem that led you to need the money is still there.

COMPETITION

The main argument that has been used to justify privatisation is that competition brings advantages. A business in competition must keep low prices and high standards of service in order to attract customers. Some denationalised businesses, such as British Airways or Sealink, face very obvious competition, but they also did *before* they were denationalised. British Telecom was denationalised in 1984, and at the same time Mercury was licensed to provide direct competition with British Telecom. Together, the two companies form a **duopoly**, but very few households have a Mercury 'phone. The fact that British Telecom already had most British households connected to its network made it very difficult for a new entrant to compete.

Similarly, households in Plymouth do not have much of a choice as to whether they will buy their electricity from the South West Electricity Board or Northern Electric. It would be impractical to have a series of switches in your house so that you could choose the company from which you will buy electricity, and it would be far too expensive for Northern Electric to transport power to just one customer in Plymouth. Regional electricity companies, as with British Gas and the water companies, thus have a **natural monopoly**. Having said that, in 1998, experiments began to offer consumers the opportunity to buy their power from different regions, but such a product still has to be carried down pipelines owned and operated by the local company.

IF I SWITCH, WHAT'S INVOLVED?

First, shop around. Check for the best price and other services that rival companies are offering. Make sure the one you choose best suits your circumstances.

Once you have made your choice, you will agree a new contract with your new gas company. The contract is a legal document. Once it is signed you must give 28 days written notice to cancel it if you decide to change to another company. If an uninvited sales person comes to your home and you sign a contract, you will have 7 days to change your mind and let them know you wish to cancel.

You should only sign one contract to supply gas to your home – two competing firms cannot supply gas at the same time to the same meter. If you have more than one house you can, of course, have a different gas company to supply each.

If you decide to switch to a new company, quoting your meter point reference number (which can be found on your gas bill) will make changing a lot easier.

Your new company will read your meter, or ask you to do it for them, within two working days before or after they start to supply your gas. This reading will be used to produce a final bill from your previous company.

If possible, keep a note of your meter reading on the day you transfer to the new company.

Ofgas (the gas regulator)

Therefore, denationalisation has done only a little to increase competition. Indeed, the government has recognised this by the appointment of *regulators* who have to approve the prices set by privatised monopolies. OFWAT oversees the water industry, while OFTEL does the same for telecommunications.

PARTY PRIVATISATION POLICIES, AS AT THE 1997 GENERAL ELECTION

CONSERVATIVE

As this party regarded the privatisation programme as a success, it was to continue with the sell-off of London Underground.

LABOUR

The Conservative privatisations of 1979–87 were not to be reversed. Indeed, further privatisations were not to be ruled out.

Regulators were to be more open in their operations, and to draw up clear performance targets for utility companies, with penalties for failure.

LIBERAL DEMOCRAT

Railtrack would be taken back into the public sector. A single Office of Utility Regulation would replace the separate regulators and impose a tighter control on profits. There would be public hearings whenever utilities wished to raise prices. Regulators would have greater powers but would also be more open.

SUMMARY

- Privatisation covers a range of policies aimed at increasing the private-sector provision of services and reducing the public sector.
- Privatisation is the reverse of nationalisation which is the transfer of businesses from the private to the public sector.
- The Conservative governments of 1979–97 claimed that privatisation increases efficiency, providing businesses with an incentive to keep costs down and standards of service high.
- The problem of natural monopolies has been addressed by the establishment of regulators.
- Throughout the 1980s and 1990s, the Labour Party opposed each privatisation carried out by the Conservatives, but in government it has decided that *renationalisation* would be a waste of public funds and is therefore concentrating on stronger regulation.

Activity

Of which type of privatisation is each of the following an example?
- the sale of British Rail
- the use of Group 4 Security to transport prisoners to court
- the sale of land owned by local councils
- allowing other airlines to fly on routes once reserved for British Airways.

STUDY GUIDES

Revision Hints

You should understand why businesses were nationalised in the first place. This is a topic where you can use lots of examples. Make notes on the various methods of privatisation, and learn an example for each one. This is a very important section because the policy of privatisation is the one that is most closely associated with Mrs Thatcher. However, it was her successor John Major who went even further than she was willing to contemplate in the privatisations of the 1990s.

Exam Hints

Exam questions tend to concentrate on the characteristics of Thatcherism, and after 1983 privatisation was the key policy. However, you may be asked just how Thatcherite was John Major's government, and his continued programme of privatisation would provide good evidence.

Similarly, New Labour's abandonment of nationalisation and possible embrace of further privatisation could be seen as offering evidence that New Labour has abandoned socialism.

Practice Questions

1 'The privatisation programme of the 1980s and 1990s had more to do with public finances than with ideology.' Discuss.
2 Discuss the proposition that nationalisation is dead.

5

INFLATION

Introduction

IN THIS CHAPTER we will see that inflation has been a problem for the British economy for many years, and that this problem is intensified by the fact that while the pattern of inflation in Britain follows that of other European countries, in Britain it also tends to be at a higher level. We will see that governments (both Labour and Conservative) have tried a number of tactics to 'squeeze inflation out of the system', and that public expectations of inflation play a vital role in the success of these policies.

Key Points
- What is inflation?
- Is inflation a problem?
- Real prices and interest rates.
- Causes of inflation.
- Monetarism – a brief experiment.
- Cures for inflation.
- Inflation policies.

WHAT IS INFLATION?

Inflation is a rise in the general level of prices, so that after a period of time, you will need more money to buy the same amount of goods. (See Table 3 for some Europe-wide inflation figures.) This does not mean that *all* prices have to rise. If the inflation rate is 5 per cent, then in general, prices over the last year have risen by 5 per cent. Some prices may have risen by 2 per cent or not at all, while others may have risen by 20 per cent. The 5 per cent represents a sort of average, but this must be qualified.

Table 3: *Inflation (percentage) by country*									
YEAR	EUROPE 15*	BELGIUM	DENMARK	GERMANY	GREECE	SPAIN	FRANCE	IRELAND	ITALY	UK
1970	4.9	2.5	6.6	3.9	3.1	6.1	5.0	12.4	5.0	5.9
1972	6.4	5.4	8.2	5.6	3.3	7.7	6.3	9.7	6.3	6.5
1974	14.8	12.8	15.0	7.5	23.5	17.7	14.8	15.7	21.4	17
1976	11.6	7.8	9.9	4.2	13.4	16.4	9.9	20.1	17.8	15.7
1978	9.1	4.2	9.2	2.7	12.8	19.1	9.1	8.2	13.2	9.5
1980	13.2	6.4	10.7	5.8	21.9	15.7	13.3	1.6	20.4	16.3
1982	10.6	7.8	10.2	4.9	20.7	14.6	11.5	14.9	17.0	8.7
1984	7.4	5.7	6.4	2.4	17.9	11.9	7.7	7.3	12.1	5
1986	3.8	0.7	2.9	–0.3	22.1	9.4	2.7	3.7	6.2	4
1988	3.9	1.5	4.0	1.4	14.2	5.0	2.6	4.0	5.7	5
1990	4.8	3.5	2.7	2.8	19.9	6.5	2.8	2.0	5.9	5.5
1992	4.7	2.0	2.0	4.8	15.0	6.4	2.4	2.5	5.6	4.7
1994	3.2	3.0	1.7	2.7	10.8	4.9	1.8	2.7	4.6	2.5
1996	2.6	2.0	1.8	1.6	8.3	3.6	1.8	2.3	4.1	2.7

*Average of 15 countries in European Union

SOURCE: EUROSTAT

A simple average of all prices is not useful, because for most people, the price of a Rolls Royce car rising by 10 per cent is not as important as the price of electricity rising by just 1 per cent. Therefore, a measure has been devised which takes account of the relative importance of different prices. A survey is carried out at regular intervals to find out how people spend their money. This is called the *Family Expenditure Survey*. This information is used to give weightings to the goods and services which are included in the **Retail Prices Index (RPI)**. The RPI is measured each month by sending civil servants to a variety of shops all over the country. The researchers record the prices of the items in the RPI, and the results are compared with those for the previous month. The RPI change in a particular month is designed to show the change in the *cost of living* for a typical family.

If the RPI in a particular month is 3 per cent higher than for that month the year before, then the annual rate of inflation is 3 per cent. However, this does not mean that for any individual, their cost of living will have risen by 3 per cent. It depends on the individual's pattern of spending.

IS INFLATION A PROBLEM?

Inflation has been with us for a very long time. Throughout history, prices have been rising, and at times of crisis such as the Napoleonic Wars of the early nineteenth century (see the diagram below), prices increase very rapidly.

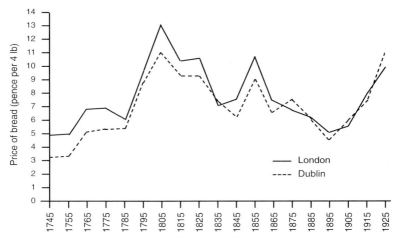

AVERAGE PRICES OF BREAD IN LONDON AND DUBLIN, 1745–1925, IN PENCE PER 4 LB

We will see later that policies used to reduce the rate of inflation include increasing interest rates or taxes. In view of the unpopularity of such measures, people often question the need to control inflation. There is indeed a range of opinions as to how important the control of inflation should be.

People argue that constantly changing prices are a great inconvenience. It is suggested that people on fixed incomes such as pensioners lose out, and this is true if the pension is not linked to the rate of inflation. In fact, Britain's state retirement pension is adjusted each year in line with the RPI. People with savings may lose out, but not if they have a savings account where the rate of interest is greater than the inflation rate (known as a *positive rate of interest*).

The two problems of inflation that cannot be avoided are as follows. First, many of you will have studied in history the problem of when inflation runs out of control (known as *hyperinflation*). Here, money becomes virtually worthless, as happened in 1920s Germany (when it was cheaper to wallpaper the house in money than to buy the wallpaper), and people will look for alternatives to money. They will switch to swapping goods for other goods, and the convenience of money will then be lost. Alternatively, they may give up on their national currency and seek to use a foreign currency, as in 1990s Russia where the US dollar is more acceptable than the Russian rouble. In Russia, the annual rate of inflation ran at 2,200 per cent in 1992. This was bad, but it only represents 25–30 per cent a month. Hyperinflation is defined as 50 per cent a month, and so Russia has a little way to go before it reaches the heights of some Latin American countries.

Activity

- What do you think are the problems for the average Russian of an annual inflation rate of 2,200 per cent?

HONESTY DOESN'T PAY

In the hyper-inflation that attended the collapse of the Soviet Union in 1991 they had lost everything.

'If you are honest in Russia the chances are that your family will go hungry.' They had picked themselves up and started again, saving enough in the '90s to put them back on their feet and allow them to think, cautiously, about retiring.

And now they could see it all beginning to happen again.

And there was one theme he kept returning to again and again: we are honest people, he kept saying, we have worked honestly and earned honest money and this is our reward.

Russia's crisis is not only economic and political, it is moral. The whole country can see that honesty, adherence to civic virtues brings no reward.

If you are honest in Russia the chances are that your family will go hungry this winter or your children will not be educated. And there is not just economic hardship in this, there is humiliation, too.

The dishonest, on the other hand, thrive here.

BBC, 8 September 1998

Second, there is the problem of loss of competitiveness. Even at relatively low levels of inflation, if prices in country A are rising more quickly than prices in country B, then eventually it will become cheaper for citizens of country A to buy their goods from country B, leading to unemployment in country A. The only way to avoid this situation would be if the exchange rate were to change. While British inflation has followed the pattern of that in other countries, namely that of being high when inflation in Europe is generally high and low when European inflation levels are generally low, Britain's inflation rate has consistently exceeded that of countries such as Germany. (Look at Table 3.)

REAL PRICES AND INTEREST RATES

Since prices are continually rising, making comparisons between price levels in different years is very difficult. To get over this, economists use the expression **real prices**. For example, if a computer cost £1,000 in 1990, and cost £1,100 in 1993, its price would have risen by 10 per cent. However, if prices generally had risen by 12 per cent in that same period of time, the computer would be relatively *cheaper* in 1993 than it had been in 1990, so its real price would have *fallen*.

Similarly, if interest rates are 6 per cent but prices are rising at 4 per cent, the extra spending power that the interest rate gives is only 2 per cent, so the real rate of interest is 2 per cent. In September 1998, the British base rate (the figure set by the Bank of England) was 7.5 per cent, while inflation was only 2.5 per cent, thus signifying a real interest rate of 5 per cent. This was historically very high.

CAUSES OF INFLATION

COST-PUSH INFLATION

The simplest explanation of inflation is called *cost-push*. This says that an increase in costs is passed on to the consumer in the form of higher prices. These cost increases could come from a rise in the price of something used in the production process, such as power or a raw material, or it could be brought about by a rise in wages or a desire for increased profits.

As wages are often a large component of a firm's costs, an increase in wages can lead to an increase in prices. If this happens on a wide scale, prices generally will rise, and workers will see that their wages now buy less. They are then likely to seek further wage rises, leading in turn to more price increases. This is called a *wage–price spiral*. A solution to this is an **incomes policy** which limits pay increases. This has been tried by successive governments in the 1960s and 1970s, but it is difficult for a government to dictate pay-increase limits to the private sector.

LABOUR'S INCOMES POLICY OF THE LATE 1960S

The TUC [Trades Union Congress] was unable to force union members to do as it said by restricting their pay demands, while the government proved incapable of keeping inflation down or producing the rapid economic expansion it had promised.

A wave of unofficial strikes was followed by employment secretary Barbara Castle's proposals to reform unions' industrial activity, *In Place of Strife*. A TUC conference rejected it.

BBC, October 1998

DEMAND-PULL INFLATION

Inflation can still occur even without increases in costs. A second cause of inflation is called *demand-pull*. Prices are determined by the interaction of two things: supply, ie how much a producer is willing to produce for sale at a particular price, and demand, ie how much customers are willing to buy at a particular price. An increase in costs will change supply: the producer will now sell less at any particular price or charge more for the same quantity.

Remember that demand is constantly changing. People's tastes and preferences change. Advertising affects the behaviour of consumers. An increase in people's incomes will lead to a greater demand for goods and services. When demand for a good or service increases and supply remains the same, the price of that good or service will increase. If there is a rise in the demand for things generally, then there will be a general rise in prices, ie demand-pull inflation.

But there is a small cloud on this horizon. The low inflation picture is dependent on the relatively high value of sterling. That makes life difficult for manufacturing industry – pushing up the price of exports and making imports cheaper. While that slows the economy down, it does so in just the wrong way.

It would be far more desirable – for the long term – to squeeze domestic consumption of one kind or another, than exports. The policy necessary to achieve this rebalancing of economic policy is one which seeks to slow the economy down while lowering the exchange rate.

Unfortunately, the only device able to effect such a trick is to reduce the government deficit – by quite a few billion – and to leave interest rates at a lower level than you otherwise would have. Low interest rates would make the pound less attractive than it would otherwise be, and that would thus see its value fall somewhat in foreign exchange markets. This is clearly the first difficult challenge of an incoming government, because there are few votes to be won in making tough decisions about the public finances.

Evan Davies, BBC Newsnight, *April 1997*

The theory of **monetarism** involves a special case of demand-pull inflation. Monetarists argue that it is the amount of money in circulation that determines the level of inflation. They believe that if the amount of money to spend increases while the number of things on which to spend it remains constant, then the average level of prices will rise. This is self-evidently true. However, the economy is never static. Therefore, inflation, for the monetarist, is caused by the increase in the money supply occurring faster than the increase in the production of goods and services.

We have found that controlling the supply of money is about as simple as getting a grip on a healthy well-greased conger eel.

Anthony Harris, The Financial Times, *8 June 1985*

Actually, there are considerable difficulties in measuring the money supply. In economics, M0, M1, M2, M3 etc are not motorways! They are differing measures of the amount of money in circulation, ranging from just notes and coins (narrow money) to measures including also bank and savings accounts and credit-card balances (broad money). Choosing the correct measure became so complicated that the monetarist government of Mrs Thatcher abandoned its practice of deciding how much the money supply should increase each year in the mid-1980s. They had never been able to get it right, because although the government can determine the issue of notes and coins, it cannot control the banking system effectively. This is because banks are free to lend, and if customers cannot borrow from British banks, they will turn to either foreign banks or other lenders.

MONETARISM – A BRIEF EXPERIMENT

During the 1970s, there was a sea change in public attitudes to the economy which expressed itself in two propositions both articulated by the Conservative Party leader Margaret Thatcher. One proposition was that low inflation rather than low unemployment should be the main aim of government policy. The second was that the government had become too big and too interventionist; that the pursuit of consensus between government, employers and trade unions which had characterised the 1960s and 1970s had led to an inefficient corporate state: a state that represents interest groups rather than individuals. It was asserted that the free operation of market forces had been hindered, and on arrival in Downing Street in 1979, Mrs Thatcher vowed to 'roll back the frontiers of the state'.

During the first part of Mrs Thatcher's (Baroness Thatcher as she is now called) premiership, the government concentrated on trying to control the money supply. At the heart of this was Nigel Lawson's (then a junior minister at the Treasury) Medium Term Financial Strategy (MTFS) which had a four-year horizon, designed to be rolled on one year forward as each year elapsed. Underlying the MTFS was the belief that inflation is caused by the money supply growing more quickly than the output of the economy, and that growth in the money supply is caused by the government's borrowing from banks to finance its *budget deficit* (ie where its spending exceeds its tax revenue).

There was a basic problem with this belief. The first was that the whole argument that an increase in the money supply causes inflation is rather suspect. If the total output of the British economy could rise by 3 per cent a year, then according to monetarism, a stable price level (ie where there is no inflation at all) would be achieved by increasing the money supply by 3 per cent a year. However, between 1980 and 1986, the government's preferred measure of the money supply, sterling M3, actually increased by 17 per cent a year. Therefore, according to the monetarist theory, inflation in 1986 should have been around 14 per cent, ie a 17 per cent increase in the money supply minus a 3 per cent growth in the economy.

By the mid-1980s, it was obvious that the rapid fall in inflation had much more to do with the fall in aggregate demand associated with the early-1980s recession when a third of the British manufacturing industry disappeared and unemployment tripled. This was the result of the high interest rates which had been set in an effort to control the money supply (or, in effect, to control the demand for money, as the point was to encourage saving and discourage borrowing). Monetarism was to all intents and purposes abandoned, and the government started to worry once more about how quickly aggregate demand would increase.

CURES FOR INFLATION

To control cost-push inflation, there is an obvious need to control costs. This is very difficult as many costs are outside the control of any country. An increase in the price of imports, used as raw materials, will often lead to cost-push inflation.

However, during the 1970s, governments did target wages as a cost that could be controlled. Incomes policies were used to limit pay claims. These policies were usually successful for about two years. After that, workers tended to push for pay claims outside the range of the policy. In Britain this led to the 1978/79 'Winter of Discontent'. If workers go on strike, an employer is faced with the same decision as if there were no incomes policy: to settle the disagreement or to cease production. For a private firm, a government may be able to impose financial or legal sanctions on any such firm that contravenes a pay policy. However, in the public sector (ie with people employed by central or local government), a government may be faced with the collapse of essential services.

The cause of demand-pull inflation is an increase in general demand that is not matched by an increase in supply. The technical term for this general level of demand, as we have seen, is *aggregate demand*, and this, again as noted before, is made up of all consumption (buying by individuals), investment (buying by businesses), government spending and surpluses of exports over imports. If a government wishes to reduce this type of inflation, it must adopt policies which will reduce aggregate demand. There are two types of policy that will achieve this. One is known as fiscal policy: anything to do with changes in tax rates or government spending. The second is called monetary policy: changes in interest rates which are carried out on the say-so of the Monetary Committee of the Bank of England.

One example of fiscal policy is that of raising income tax. Putting up income tax will leave people with less money to spend on goods and services and thus reduce demand. (Raising taxes or interest rates serves to reduce demand for goods and services.) Firms will then be left with less money to invest in new equipment. This policy will be unpopular, and may be politically problematic for a government elected on the promise to reduce taxes. Cutting government spending would also reduce the demand for goods and services, but again this will be unpopular with those groups especially affected by such cuts.

Whereas Keynesians believe that the main influences on the price level are external factors such as trade union power, monetarists believe that the 'given' factor is the level of employment which the economy is capable of providing at any one time. In other words for Keynesians a boost to demand (and thus an increase in the money supply) will mainly affect output while for monetarists its main effect will be on prices.

Adapted from The Times, *24 August 1987*

Then how might monetary policy work? Increasing interest rates has an effect on business in that they are now less likely to borrow money to invest since the interest payments will be greater, making the investment decision less profitable. However, the biggest effect is on consumption. Individuals would be less likely to purchase large items for which they may need loans, and so demand will fall.

The biggest impact is brought about by the fact that a very large number of households (especially in Britain and the USA) have mortgages. When the interest rate rises, mortgage payers are faced with larger repayments each month. They are then left with less disposable income, ie money to spend on goods and services. On the other hand, savers receive more interest, but they are likely to keep this in their accounts rather than spend it.

The effect of reducing aggregate demand is a reduction in the demand for goods and services, and a reduction in the number of firms and people needed to provide goods and services. The economy is likely to go into a recession (defined as six months of continued decline in the country's output), with high levels of unemployment, as we shall see in the next chapter.

INFLATION POLICIES

The accepted wisdom of the last two decades of the twentieth century has been that inflation is public enemy number one. Mrs Thatcher put its defeat at the top of her agenda, and Nigel Lawson (Chancellor of the Exchequer for much of the 1980s) said that the inflation rate would be 'judge and jury' of his monetary policy.

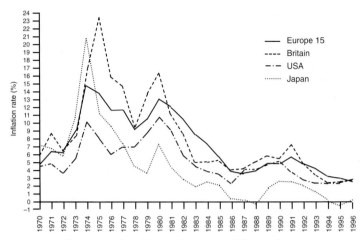

INFLATION RATES (PERCENTAGE) FOR EUROPE, BRITAIN, THE USA AND JAPAN

SOURCE: EUROSTAT

Although the general trend was for inflation to rise in the 1970s and fall in the 1980s, the phenomenon was particularly acute for Britain (see the diagram above). Under the 1974–79 Labour government, inflation peaked at 26.9 per cent in August 1975. Under Mrs Thatcher, the highest rate was 21.9 per cent in May 1980. A common belief was that Mrs Thatcher brought prices down, but in fact in every year of her premiership prices actually rose, though it is true that after 1980 the speed of the rise, ie the *rate of inflation*, did slow down (see again the diagram above).

During the 1992–97 Parliament, inflation was generally low – the smallest figure being 1.2 per cent in June 1993 and the highest 3.9 per cent in September 1994.

Interest rates serve to regulate aggregate demand, and one of the first acts of Chancellor Gordon Brown on coming to office in May 1997 was to hand over the responsibility for setting interest rates from the Treasury (the Chancellor of the Exchequer's Department) to the Monetary Committee of the Bank of England. The Bank of England was given the target for inflation of 2.5 per cent – the same as that set by the previous Chancellor Kenneth Clarke – and then left to get on with it. It is hoped that, free from political pressures, the Bank of England will have more credibility with politicians in handling this objective. It was widely believed that the previous Conservative Chancellor Kenneth Clarke avoided raising interest rates when the Bank of England was calling for them to rise in early 1987 because it would be unpopular before an election. High interest rates are indeed politically unpopular, but then so is high inflation.

The IMF warned the current slowdown might see the UK's inflation target overshot.

'The possibility of a sharper slowdown than needed to meet the inflation target, warrants readiness for an early move toward monetary easing,' the report said.

The report said that although unemployment has fallen to an 18-year low, wages growth has moderated as Britain tries to meet its inflation target of 2.5 per cent.

The Bank of England has said rising wages have been the main factor holding up interest rates in recent months.

But the IMF said: 'Significant fiscal consolidation, together with the tightening of monetary policy should help to contain inflation risks in the period ahead.'

The IMF's *World Economic Outlook* report forecast British growth of 2.3 per cent this year, slowing to 1.2 per cent in 1999.

Six months ago, the fund predicted 2.3 per cent growth in 1998 and 2.2 per cent in 1999.

IMF chief economist Michael Mussa said he believed the agency's growth forecasts for Britain were a 'pretty good central estimate'.

At odds with Blair

The predictions come just as prime minister Tony Blair and chancellor Gordon Brown have firmly turned down demands by industry and Labour party conference delegates for immediate rate cuts.

They have said the brief the government gives the interest rate authority – the Bank of England's Monetary Policy Committee (MPC) – will continue to have inflation and long-term economic goals at the top of its list.

This means it won't support rate cuts to alleviate short-term pain. The MPC will hold its monthly deliberations on interest rates next week.

Thousands of jobs have been lost in manufacturing industries across the UK in recent months, with the high pound, the Asian crisis and a domestic slowdown blamed.

Analysts have joined the IMF in calling for rate cuts, saying the latest domestic figures add to downward signals in the housing and share markets.

'Falling stocks and house prices are a doubled-edged sword which mean consumers are going to be singing the blues in the next few months,' said David Brown, economist at Bear Stearns International in London.

'The MPC have got all the intellectual ammunition they need to justify a cut next week,' he said.

BBC, October 1998

SUMMARY

- Inflation is a persistent tendency for prices to rise.
- Inflation may be caused by costs being too high (cost-push) or by there being too much demand (demand-pull) in the economy for business to meet.
- Government cures for inflation involve either attempts to keep costs down or the reduction of aggregate demand, and both these have undesirable consequences.
- Inflation becomes a serious problem if people lose confidence in the currency, or domestic levels of inflation are above average so that people switch to buying the products of other countries.

Activities

1   At the beginning of a year, you have £10 to spend. During that year, the rate of inflation is 5 per cent. At the end of the year, how much money would you need to have the same spending power as you had at the beginning of the year?

2   The following inflation rates occurred in an imaginary country called Ruritania:
    a   1985: 4 per cent
    b   1986: 5 per cent
    c   1987: 9 per cent
    d   1988: 8 per cent
    e   1989: 9 per cent
    f   1990: 6 per cent.
During which years did prices fall?

See p 117 at the back of the book for answers to these Activities.

STUDY GUIDES

Revision Hints

The key to the importance of inflation for the study of government and politics is that the control of inflation has been the central plank of British government policy since the 1970s. Prior to this, low unemployment had been the central aim. This issue runs across parties, and so again, time is more important than ideology. In other words, although the Thatcher government is closely associated in the public imagination with the reduction of inflation, this had in fact been falling rapidly in three years of Labour government before she came to power. In fact, in her first year in office, inflation once again exceeded 20 per cent.

Also, remember again that while it is commonly believed that Mrs Thatcher brought down prices, the reality is that prices on average rose every year during her administration, just as they have done in every year since 1935. It was Dennis Healey, as the Labour Chancellor in 1976, who first targeted the money supply to control inflation, but he was also concerned about unemployment. Mrs Thatcher's government was much more single-minded in its attempts to control the money supply, but it was also her government that abandoned monetarism and returned to old-fashioned demand management.

Similarly, both Labour and Conservative governments of the 1960s and 1970s used an incomes policy to restrain cost-push inflation, and so there is a continuity here in economic policy.

Exam Hints

Questions tend to look at the broad sweep of changing policy, and so it is important to know the economic context. Remember that in the mid-1970s, inflation took over from unemployment as the biggest economic problem in the minds of most of the electorate. Economic circumstances have dictated a changing approach to inflation which involved targeting costs through incomes policy during the 1960s and 1970s, targeting the money supply during the period 1976–85, and finally using interest rates to control aggregate demand in the period from 1985 to the time of writing (1999).

Practice Questions

1 Why have British governments of the 1980s and 1990s seen inflation as a bigger enemy than unemployment?

2 Comment on the policies to combat inflation adopted by British governments over the last 20 years.

6

UNEMPLOYMENT

Introduction

THIS CHAPTER WILL explain what is meant by unemployment. It will examine the ways in which different governments have attempted to deal with this problem, and it will introduce you to the ideas favoured by different economists. However, while economists can suggest policies to reduce unemployment, any such policy will have both advantages and disadvantages. It is the role of the politician to actually make the decisions based on the advice of economists.

The problem of unemployment has been closely associated with that of inflation. This is because, as we shall discover in this chapter, the price of reducing unemployment is often an increase in inflation. For most of the period since 1945, governments, and particularly Chancellors of the Exchequer, have been concerned with managing the economy so as to strike a balance between *acceptable* levels of unemployment and inflation. The current (1998) Chancellor of the Exchequer Gordon Brown claims to have abandoned this approach. As we will see in Chapter 9's section on 'Welfare to Work', he is concentrating his efforts on making it easier for people to be employed, while leaving the control of inflation to the Bank of England. Whether this is actually possible, only time will tell.

Key Points
- Unemployment in Britain
- The meaning of unemployment.
- The costs of unemployment.
- Policies to reduce unemployment.

UNEMPLOYMENT IN BRITAIN

During the 1950s and 1960s, unemployment in Britain never rose above 500,000. It started a steady rise through the 1970s, but even in 1980 it was commonly believed that no government could expect to be re-elected with unemployment at over 1 million (the Labour government lost the 1979 General Election partly due to the Conservative's slogan 'Labour isn't working').

'LABOUR ISN'T WORKING': A 1979 CONSERVATIVE PARTY ELECTION ADVERT

However, the 1983 British Election proved that a government *could*, and throughout the 1980s and into the 1990s, the British economy has experienced historically high levels of unemployment. It seems that while the electorate disapproves of high levels of unemployment, other factors such as its personal economic well-being are more important in determining voting intentions. By the 1997 General Election, it seemed that rather than the absolute level of unemployment in the country affecting government support, it was more a case of job security or people's assessment of their own chances of being unemployed that contributed to the Conservative government unpopularity. Obviously, the absolute level of unemployment affects one's view of one's own chances of being unemployed, but in the early 1980s the high levels of unemployment were largely concentrated among manual workers and geographical areas away from the south-east of England. With 3 million people unemployed, and with each of these people affecting the economic well-being of two other voters in their family, that still only affects 9 million people. The vast majority of the electorate were unaffected.

By the mid-1990s, unemployment was lower than it had been in the mid-1980s peak, but it had become a risk for formerly unaffected white-collar workers, and now included all geographical areas.

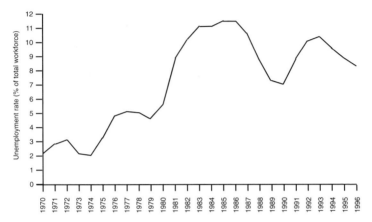

THE BRITISH UNEMPLOYMENT RATE (PERCENTAGE OF TOTAL WORKFORCE)
SOURCE: EUROSTAT

Some economists believe that the change from the low levels of unemployment in the 1950s to the much higher levels of the 1980s and 1990s was caused by a long-term problem with the supply of labour. Other economists believe that unemployment is a problem of the lack of competitiveness in British businesses caused by too little investment in machinery and too little training and education for the workforce. However, the problem of unemployment has affected most Western countries over the last two decades (see the diagram on page 55).

THE MEANING OF UNEMPLOYMENT

You may think that the meaning of unemployment is quite obvious: being without work. But think! Which of the following people, each of whom is without work, would you say is unemployed?

- Steve, aged 17, taking A levels at college and planning to go to university;
- Jo, aged 19, training to be a doctor;
- Emma, aged 24, looking after her 6-month-old baby;

- Tom, aged 58, who has just accepted early retirement but who would still like to work;
- Martin, aged 68, who would like to work but who is considered too old;
- Suzanne, aged 28, who is desperately looking for a job and who has to rely on her husband's income of £9,000.

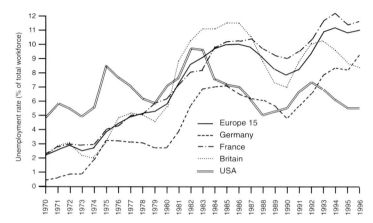

UNEMPLOYMENT RATES (PERCENTAGE OF THE WORKFORCE)
SOURCE: EUROSTAT

According to official British government statistics in force in 1998, none of the people listed above is unemployed. This is because the official British government definition of unemployment is that of people registered as seeking work and claiming benefit for being unemployed from the Department of Social Security (DSS). Both these conditions must be met. In economic theory, on the other hand, unemployment is considered to cover those people who are without a job and are prepared to accept one at existing wage rates. Tom, Martin and Suzanne above are all looking for work but are unable to claim unemployment benefit. In this way, many people believe that official measures of unemployment are underestimates.

JOBLESS COUNT 'FIDDLE' TO END

By Rachel Sylvester, Political Correspondent

Unemployment figures are to increase by more than 500,000 because the Government is changing the way that it measures the number of people out of work in order to counter charges that the statistics have been fiddled.

The Office for National Statistics announced yesterday that from April the figures will include people who have no jobs as well as those on unemployment benefit. The Government is also finalising plans to fulfil its manifesto commitment to create an independent National Statistical Service to head off criticism that figures could be manipulated for political ends. In Opposition, Labour constantly accused the Tories of 'fiddling' the monthly figures.

Under the current system, the headline statistic is based on the Claimant Count, the number of people on unemployment-related benefits – at the moment this is 1,411,200. In future, Labour Force Survey data, based on polls of households across the country, every month, will be used. At the moment this shows 1,913,000 people out of work.

Daily Telegraph, *4 February 1998*

TYPES OF UNEMPLOYMENT

Economists distinguish between different types of unemployment in the following way. First, there are two forms of unemployment that are always with us:

1 **frictional (or search) unemployment**. Most workers who leave a job move quickly to a new one. This short-term unemployment is called frictional, and it existed even during the low levels of the 1950s and 1960s.
2 **seasonal unemployment**. Some workers, such as those employed in tourism or in building, are only employed for part of the year. Such seasonal unemployment tends to rise in winter and fall in summer.

Next are some rather more worrying forms of unemployment, because they indicate weaknesses in the economy itself and have resulted in unemployment lasting longer and affecting more people than was the case in the 1950s and 1960s.

STRUCTURAL UNEMPLOYMENT

Structural unemployment occurs when changes in the structure of industry come about. For example, the steel and shipbuilding industries in Britain experienced a rapid decline during the 1970s and 1980s, and many former steelworkers and shipbuilders became unemployed. During the 1980s and 1990s, the coal industry has experienced a dramatic decline. Many villages were built as a result of the sinking of a coal mine, and so there is often no alternative employment available any longer in an area.

Structural unemployment has been present since the Industrial Revolution as new processes replace old. New industries need to employ people, but as these may not set up in the area where the old industry existed, pockets of severe unemployment may remain. This leads to regional unemployment.

Structural unemployment in Britain has been associated with primary and secondary industries based in the north of the country, so that even during the 'boom' of the mid-to-late 1980s, unemployment in northern regions remained high.

CYCLICAL UNEMPLOYMENT

Cyclical unemployment is brought about by a fall in aggregate demand. The history of the British economy has been one of increases in aggregate demand followed by decreases. Notice the pattern of booms and slumps in the economic-growth rates diagram below. This pattern (to use the term again) is what is known as *stop-go economics*, and the Chancellor of the Exchequer (Gordon Brown) is frequently quoted as saying that we do not want a return to 'stop–go'.

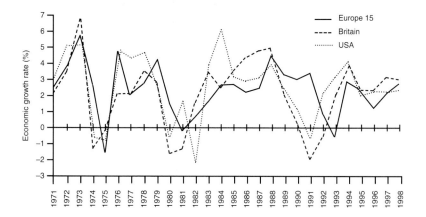

ECONOMIC GROWTH RATES (PERCENTAGE)
SOURCE: EUROSTAT

Cyclical unemployment falls when the level of aggregate demand increases, so the solution to this type of unemployment is relatively simple: increase aggregate demand. However, there are problems with increasing aggregate demand because this can lead to increases in inflation (see Chapter 5) or to a worsening in the **balance of payments** (see Chapter 7).

THE COSTS OF UNEMPLOYMENT

Unemployment has some obvious costs for the individual. They will experience a fall in income, and so their standard of living will also fall. In turn, this will reduce their family's ability to purchase what they want. The individual will also experience a loss of self-worth since people often describe themselves in terms of the job that they do; eg 'I'm an accountant', 'I'm a builder' or 'I'm a teacher'.

Being unemployed is very stressful, and the rate of suicides and ill health of most kinds is markedly higher among the unemployed than among people in work.

There are also important costs to society from unemployment. Most obviously, the unemployed receive benefit which is paid for out of taxes. Therefore, either taxes have to be higher than they otherwise would be, or government spending on other things will be reduced.

There is also a loss of government revenue, as the unemployed do not pay tax. At times of high unemployment, government spending rises while tax revenue falls, and so the Public Sector Borrowing Requirement (PSBR) increases to make up the difference. The government has to pay interest on this borrowing.

There is also a less obvious cost to society. That is the lost output that the unemployed would have produced if they had had a job. If the unemployment rate is 10 per cent and these people represent an average cross-section of the workforce, then perhaps if they were in work the country could increase its output by 10 per cent.

UNEMPLOYMENT SINCE THE 1970s

When the Conservatives campaigned in 1979, they made much of the dismal state of the labour market. They played on fears of trade-union power, which was not hard to do because the 'Winter of Discontent' (a spate of public-sector strikes in 1978–9 that led to uncollected rubbish and hospitals limited to accepting only emergency admissions) was still fresh in the public memory. The Tories scored on unemployment as well. The jobless total had hit 1 million in 1975 – during Labour's second year in office – and had not dipped below since.

After the Tories' emasculating labour laws of the early 1980s, it is no longer so easy to paint horns on the unions. According to the more recent MORI polls, only a quarter of voters believe that trade unions have too much power. In September 1978, 82 per cent did. Unemployment, though, has kept some of its political bite. In another MORI poll in February 1997, 38 per cent of voters cited it as one of the biggest issues facing Britain. Even though this is far below the 84 per cent recorded just before the General Election of 1983, unemployment still ranks high in such polls.

A glance at the dole queue shows why. Higher unemployment has become a fact of life, though not an acceptable one. In the most recent 18 years of Tory rule, the recorded rate of unemployment rose by half, even though there were several changes to the method of measurement that makes the total lower than it would otherwise have been. When the Conservatives came to office in 1979, at the peak of an economic cycle, 1.3 million Britons were on the jobless register. They amounted to 4 per cent of the workforce. During the first seven Tory years, unemployment climbed continuously, peaking at around 3.4 million (11.1 per cent) in 1986. After the recession of the early 1990s, the rate reached 10.5 per cent in December 1992. It has been falling since early 1993, and in 1998 was 6.5 per cent.

What has not been falling is the rate of long-term unemployment. The proportion of the unemployed who have been out of work for a year or more has averaged around one-third since at least the early 1980s. Some will have given up the search for work and thus do not appear in the records. Most European countries have a similar core of long-term unemployed. In Germany in 1995, for example, 48 per cent of the jobless had been out of work for more than a year, compared with 44 per cent in Britain.

Britain's overall unemployment figures mask an undulating landscape of hills and valleys. The largest regional jobless rates have traditionally been found mainly in Ulster, the north of England, Scotland and Wales. In the early 1990s, though, there was some levelling out: south-east England took the brunt of a recession which hit service industries particularly hard. But now the south-east is doing relatively better again. Scottish unemployment is now 7.1 per cent compared with 6 per cent in the south-east.

The type of work available, and who is doing it, has changed in three main ways during the Tory years:

1 The shift in employment from manufacturing to services, which began early this century, has continued apace. Service-sector employment already accounted for 14 million jobs, or 60 per cent of the total, in 1979. Now, 17 million people, or 75 per cent of those in work, earn their living in what are classed as services. The largest categories in this group of jobs are retailing, property, health care and social work. Although manufacturing employment has risen a little in the past few years, it now provides about 4 million jobs, compared with 6.7 million in 1979. The growth of the service sector is mirrored in other industrialised nations. Even in Germany, where the service sector's share of employment has traditionally been smaller than in other Group of Seven rich countries, the proportion of workers in service industries has risen from 50 per cent to 59 per cent since 1979.

2 The share of jobs filled by women also continues to grow. Although both male and female employment have risen and fallen with the jobs cycle, over the long term, the number of working women has grown while the number of male workers has shrunk. In 1979, women accounted for 39 per cent of all employment; now their share is almost half. The proportion of working-age women who are employed has risen from 56 per cent to 63 per cent since 1979.

3 The Conservatives' period in office has coincided with a rise in part-time work. Indeed, the increase in the number of part-time jobs explains pretty much all of Britain's recent job creation. In 1996, total employment was up by 640,000 on 1980; but the number of part-time jobs had risen from 4.6 million to 6.4 million. Almost half of all women's jobs are now part-time ones, compared with 42 per cent of a smaller total in 1991. In 1996, 1.3 million men worked part-time. In 1981, the figure was only 738,000.

The Conservatives have long argued that a flexible labour market is the key to creating jobs and attracting foreign investment. It proudly contrasts Britain's record with that of other European countries in which stiffer labour-market regulations apply. Britain's unemployment rate is currently lower than those in Europe's other big economies: in France, for instance, the rate is 12.7 per cent; in Germany, it is 10.9 per cent; in Italy, 12.2 per cent; and in Spain, 21.9 per cent. In the European Union (EU), only the Netherlands and Portugal do better. Britain's record on labour costs, though, is mixed. According to the Organisation for Economic Cooperation and Development (OECD), in 1983–93 Britain's unit labour costs rose by an average of 5.4 per cent a year; in the EU as a whole, the rate was 4 per cent.

Some deep differences remain between the two main parties' views of Britain's labour market. The Conservatives are more prepared than Labour to treat it like any other market, hence their focus on deregulation and their opposition to the idea of a minimum wage and to the Maastricht Social Chapter. Yet in the past couple of years, both parties have trimmed their philosophies.

(This section has been adapted from *The Economist Election Briefing 1997*.)

Table 4: *Key landmarks in unemployment figures in Britain*	
1976	Registered unemployment passes 1 million for the first time since the Second World War. Following this shock, the levels fall back to below 1 million again by 1979.
1981	Registered unemployment passes 2 million for the first time since the Second World War.
1984	Registered unemployment passes 3 million for the first time since the Second World War.

UNEMPLOYMENT POLICY AT THE 1997 GENERAL ELECTION

- Conservative: more flexible working practices to promote job creation. Work experience for the long-term unemployed. The modern apprenticeships scheme to improve on-job vocational training to be expanded, as would be vocational qualifications.
- Labour: windfall tax revenue targeted at getting 250,000 under-25-year-olds off benefit and into work. Benefits scheme personalised so as to tackle fraud. Skills raised by guaranteeing workers access to 'Learn As You Earn' accounts to finance training. Employers offered a £75-a-week tax rebate for six months when employing someone who has been jobless for over two years. A University of Industry to provide training.

- Liberal Democrat: introduction to a 'Benefit Transfer Programme': employers would receive a £150 training voucher to take on the long-term unemployed and pay the going rate for the job. National insurance contributions reduced for the long-term unemployed. Those who employ under-19s would have to release them for a minimum of two days' training a week.

POLICIES TO REDUCE UNEMPLOYMENT

THE CLASSICAL APPROACH

The classical view of unemployment is that it is caused by the market for labour's experiencing more supply than demand. Let us think about the market for peaches. When there is a good harvest of peaches and there are a lot about, stores will be anxious to sell a lot of peaches, and so they will cut their prices. If they did not do this, then the normal number of peaches would be sold and the extra amount would be left to rot. Classical economists believe that labour has a market just as do goods such as peaches. If average wage rates are too high, firms will not employ as many workers as there are workers seeking jobs. The difference between the number of people wanting to work at any wage rate and the number of workers that firms are willing to take on is what determines the level of unemployment. According to this analysis, unemployment will be reduced by workers' accepting jobs at lower wage rates. However, unlike peaches, wages are 'downwardly sticky'. In other words, contracts of employment make it difficult for firms to reduce the wage rate offered for a particular job, when there are cheaper supplies of labour available.

FOLLY OF THE LEFT-WING CLAMOUR FOR MINIMUM WAGES

By Roland Gribben, Business Editor

As the Lille G7 summit on unemployment unfolded, one could definitely hear the murmuring of mea culpa from the European delegations – sotto voce of course. Europe – the continent, that is – has an unemployment problem that is rapidly becoming a crisis, and may soon become a catastrophe. Unemployment there is more than 11 pc and rising; and there is diminishing hope that the expected recovery in late 1996 will do much to flow that rise. Already the more honest politicians are admitting to second thoughts on monetary union, previously seen as their sneaky back door to political union.

Perhaps even more significantly, they are pointing to the European 'Social Model' as the root cause of the unemployment problem; and are deeply worried by that diagnosis. While it may indeed be the cause, how they wonder can they tell their voters, who are now addicted to minimum wages, employment protection, strong unions with power to strike at any time and, to cap it all in Germany, the pure farce of a week's obligatory paid holiday in a spa? The political imperative confronts the politically impossible. There is a timely lesson here for Tony Blair, as he shapes his still-veiled platform for the coming election. He is, as things stand, committed to bringing in a minimum wage and to signing the Social Chapter. Yet the continental debacle is a grim warning.

Daily Telegraph, *9 April 1996*

How will the introduction of the minimum wage to the UK in 1999 affect unemployment?

THE KEYNESIAN APPROACH

The Keynesian approach to reducing unemployment has been to adopt policies aimed at increasing aggregate demand. Therefore, the government in this case should either increase government spending, reduce taxes or reduce interest rates.

SURPRISE JOBLESS RISE 'VINDICATES' BASE RATE CUT

By Anne Segall, Economics Correspondent

The number of people registered as unemployed rose by an unexpected 6,800 last month, taking the seasonally adjusted count to 2,213,600, the first rise for two-and-a-half years.

Analysts responded favourably, claiming that in the light of the latest labour market figures the decision by the Chancellor Kenneth Clarke to cut bank base rates from 6.25pc to 6pc a week ago appeared 'fully vindicated'. David Walton said he expected the data 'to bring the recent period of gilt market underperformance to an end'.

The Daily Telegraph, *14 March 1996*

How may these interest rate adjustments affect the level of unemployment?

SUPPLY-SIDE THEORY (THE CURRENT ORTHODOXY)

However, other economists, known as *supply-siders*, believe that policies to increase aggregate demand can only be successful for a short period of time and are harmful in the long term because they lead to inflation. They believe in something called the **natural rate of employment**. This is the proportion of the workforce that remains unemployed when the labour market is in equilibrium. In other words, various problems exist to prevent the unemployed from accepting jobs at the sort of wage rates where firms would be willing to take on more staff. These problems, and appropriate solution are as follows:

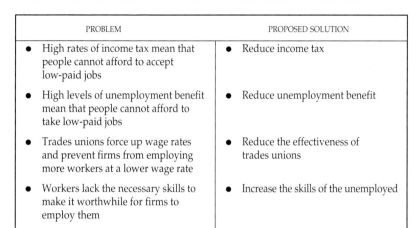

PROBLEM	PROPOSED SOLUTION
● High rates of income tax mean that people cannot afford to accept low-paid jobs	● Reduce income tax
● High levels of unemployment benefit mean that people cannot afford to take low-paid jobs	● Reduce unemployment benefit
● Trades unions force up wage rates and prevent firms from employing more workers at a lower wage rate	● Reduce the effectiveness of trades unions
● Workers lack the necessary skills to make it worthwhile for firms to employ them	● Increase the skills of the unemployed

The natural rate of unemployment is more formally known as the *non-accelerating inflation rate of unemployment* (NAIRU). This is the level of unemployment which can be maintained without increasing the inflation rate.

Rather than use aggregate-demand increases to reduce the level of unemployment, the British Conservative government of 1979–97 tried to adopt the policies listed above. However, the data shown in the diagram below illustrates that actual reductions in unemployment have been followed by increases in aggregate demand while increases in unemployment have been closely associated with falls in demand.

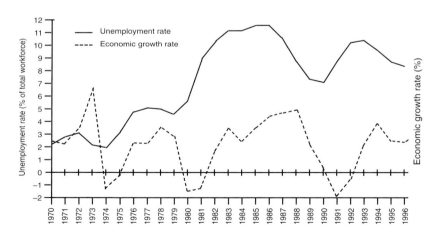

<small>British unemployment rates (percentage of total workforce) and economic-growth rates (percentage)</small>
SOURCE: EUROSTAT

SUMMARY

There is a range of views as to who should be counted as unemployed and therefore what constitutes the level of unemployment. Unemployment can be caused by too little aggregate demand in the economy. It can also be a supply problem, with workers unwilling or unable to accept jobs at the wage rates being offered. It can also result from changes in the pattern of industry in an economy, eg the move from manufacturing to services.

The appropriate government policy will depend on the type of unemployment involved. The government in 1999 is chiefly concerned with helping the victims of structural unemployment to find jobs. Critics argue that *back-to-work* policies are only effective if there are job vacancies to be filled, and these will only exist if there is sufficient demand for goods and services in the economy.

Revision Hints

You will need to be familiar with the content of this chapter and with the 'Welfare to Work' section in Chapter 9.

Make sure you understand why unemployment is not just a problem for the individual but has costs for the whole country.

Make sure also that you understand that unemployment can be caused by a problem with the supply of labour: a skill mismatch, eg lots of former coal miners untrained to take on jobs in service industries; or by a lack of demand for workers in the economy.

Exam Hints

Remember that this is not an economics exam, and so you need not explain in detail the interaction of supply and demand in the labour market. Rather, you need to concentrate on the different policies from which governments may choose, and remember that during the 1950s and 1960s unemployment in Britain never rose above 500,000. Unemployment started a steady rise through the 1970s, but even in 1980 it was commonly believed that no government could expect to be re-elected with unemployment at over 1 million. Mass unemployment has been a phenomenon of the 1980s and 1990s. A relatively low level in the late 1990s would have been a shocking level in the 1960s.

You may well need to combine information from the last chapter on inflation with information on unemployment because it is through the regulation of aggregate demand that both are affected.

Practice Questions

1 **a** How and why were Keynesian economic policies abandoned?
   b What have been the major effects of this policy shift?
2 How can governments reduce the level of unemployment?

7

INTERNATIONAL TRADE AND EXCHANGE RATES

Introduction

IN 1947, 23 countries signed the General Agreement on Tariffs and Trade (GATT). This was in response to the view that previous wars had often been caused by countries failing to trade with one another. The GATT rules prevented member countries from increasing restrictions on trade with one another, and since 1947 new GATT agreements have sought to reduce trade restrictions between countries and to encourage world trade.

Some areas of the world have sought to greatly reduce trade barriers to a point where they do not exist, eg the European Union, but this has only applied to member countries, while restrictions on imports from outside a particular group of countries have been strictly enforced.

In this chapter, we will see that international trade has been shown to be beneficial to countries. However, there are times when governments perceive a need to restrict trade. We will explore an issue that has vital importance to British business, namely that it is exchange rates which determine how much a business's exports will cost abroad and how much in turn imports will cost in Britain. We will see that there have been times when the exchange rate has been fixed to give business some stability. However, the last time that this was tried ended in the political disaster of Black Wednesday.

Key Points
- Comparative advantage.
- Restricting international trade.

- The meaning of exchange rates.
- How are exchange rates determined?
- The effects of exchange-rate changes.
- Fixed and floating exchange rates.
- The European Monetary System.

COMPARATIVE ADVANTAGE

Adam Smith is often thought of as the father of modern economics. In his book *The Wealth of Nations* (1776), a famous example is given. It is shown how in a pin factory, the processes involved in producing a pin are split up so that different workers specialised in different tasks. The principle of *division of labour*, namely that output can be increased through specialisation, can also be applied to countries. Suppose that just two countries decide to trade with each other, and that they only trade two goods, bread and sausages:

	NUMBER OF MAN HOURS to PRODUCE 1 UNIT OF:	
	BREAD	SAUSAGES
Britain	3	2
France	2	4

Here, France has an *absolute advantage* in the production of bread because it takes only 2 man hours to make a unit of bread in France whereas in Britain it takes 3. On the other hand, Britain has an absolute advantage in the production of sausages. Thus, if Britain were to import all its bread from France and divert the resources that it once used to make bread to making sausages, while France gave up making sausages and concentrated on bread, both countries would be better off.

However, even in a situation where one country has an absolute advantage in the production of both goods, it may still be advantageous to both countries for them both to specialise. Let's assume that Ruritania is more efficient than Caladonia in the production of both the above goods: it has an absolute advantage in bread and sausages. The principle still works as long as the *opportunity costs* involved, defined as the costs in terms of *the best alternatives foregone*, differ. For example, assume that with a certain amount of resources, Caladonia can produce either 20 sausages or 200 loaves of bread, and that with the same level of resources, Ruritania can produce either 10 sausages or 150 loaves of bread. In terms of resources used, the costs of production for *both* products is lower in Caladonia. However, if we look at the opportunity cost, a different picture emerges. In

Caladonia, the cost of 1 sausage is 10 loaves of bread, while in Ruritania it is 15 loaves of bread. In terms of the number of sausages given up to make bread, bread is therefore cheaper to make in Ruritania. Ruritania, we say, has a *comparative advantage* in bread.

RESTRICTING INTERNATIONAL TRADE

Having looked at the advantages of international trade, we need to consider the fact that there are various restrictions on trade. These can take the following forms.

QUOTAS

A quota is a limit placed on the quantity of a good that can be imported.

VOLUNTARY EXPORT RESTRAINT

This is a fairly new development whereby a country voluntarily agrees to limit its exports of a product. For example, the EU has an agreement with Japanese car producers that the Japanese will not take more than 10 per cent of the European market for cars. This amounts to a voluntary quota adopted by the exporting country to avoid something worse being imposed by the importing country.

Both quotas and voluntary export restraints lead to consumers' having their choice limited, and to the payment of higher prices – see the diagram below.

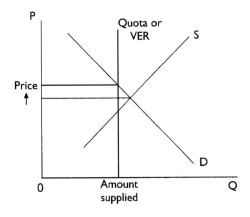

How a quota or voluntary export restraint leads to restricted supply and a higher price

TARIFFS

A *tariff* is a tax on imported goods, sometimes also called an *import duty* or a *customs duty*. Tariffs are used to discourage consumers from buying imported products by raising their price – see the diagram below. The effect is slightly different from the quota as, with a quota, the extra price benefits the producer whereas with a tariff the government gains from the extra price.

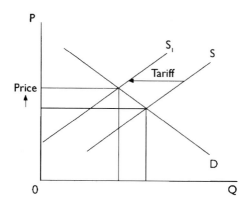

HOW A TARIFF REDUCES SUPPLY AND RAISES THE PRICE

OTHER METHODS OF RESTRICTING TRADE

Rather than adopt policies to make imported goods more expensive, a government could decide to make goods produced within the country cheaper by providing a subsidy. For example, in the mid-1990s, fares on Air France were cheaper than they otherwise might be because the French government was paying the debts of the business. In 1998, this was ruled illegal by the European Court of Justice because it was giving Air France an unfair advantage over other airlines in the European Union.

Other ways of restricting imports are by adopting *non-tariff barriers*. These can involve anything designed to make it more difficult for consumers to buy imported goods. For example, during the 1980s, the French government decided that all Japanese video machines had to be imported through a small airport hundreds of miles from Paris.

REASONS FOR TRADE RESTRICTIONS

Policies to restrict free trade are called *protection* as they are designed to protect a country's industry from foreign competition. There are a number of reasons for such policies:

- *to raise revenue.* In Britain, HM Customs and Excise has been taxing imported goods for more than 300 years. The smuggling of products such as tobacco and alcohol – which can be obtained more cheaply abroad – has a long history. However, import duties are quite insignificant in terms of overall taxation, and the money raised goes to the European Union's budget.
- *the infant industry argument.* One argument for protection in certain circumstances is that industries just starting up will not benefit from the economies of scale of the already-existing industries in other countries. Therefore, it is argued that to allow a new industry to set up in a country, it is justifiable to protect the industry from foreign competition while it is starting up. The problem is that one day, the competition from the real world will come as something of a shock.
- *to prevent dumping.* Dumping is selling a product for less than the cost of producing it. The British motorcycle industry was largely destroyed by Japanese firms exporting motorbikes to Britain and selling them for less than they cost to produce. This forced British manufacturers out of business, leaving the market open to the Japanese who could then increase prices.

The issue of how much free trade should take place has been important in British politics. In the early and mid-nineteenth century, a major realignment took place in British politics over whether the imports of corn should be restricted. Farmers favoured restricting the import of corn so that they could sell their own products. This position was supported by the Tory Party which gave rise to the modern Conservative Party. Tory supporters of free trade joined with the Whigs to form the modern Liberal Party, taking the view that restrictions on imports were a bad idea as they might lead to restrictions on our exports.

This basic argument between supporters of *free trade* and supporters of *protectionism* has resurfaced whenever Britain has faced periods of very high unemployment. Indeed, in the early 1980s, Labour's *Alternative Economic Strategy* took a protectionist line. However, in the 1990s there is a consensus among the political parties that free trade is a good idea, a consensus that does not exist in the USA.

THE MEANING OF EXCHANGE RATES

An **exchange rate** is simply the price of one currency expressed in terms of another currency (see Table 5). For example, if you are going on holiday to France, you will need to get French francs to spend while you are in that country. You will need to buy these francs at a bank before you go, on the boat during the crossing or in a bank in France. Whichever way you do it, you will have to pay for these francs in pounds, and so you will need to know how many francs you can buy for your British money. In January 1999, you could buy 9.00 French francs for £1, making the exchange rate £1 = FF 9.00.

Table 5: *Exchange rates for £1 sterling in different countries' currencies, as at 27 November 1998*

Australia	2.53	Malaysia	6.30
Austria	19.24	Malta	0.6173
Belgium	56.60	Netherlands	3.0830
Canada	2.47	New Zealand	3.04
Cyprus	0.8088	Norway	12.15
Denmark	10.48	Portugal	278.86
Finland	8.42	Saudi Arabia	6.12
France	9.1709	Singapore	2.68
Germany	2.7436	South Africa	9.28
Greece	460.32	Spain	232.12
Hong Kong	12.49	Sweden	13.23
India	70.576	Switzerland	2.266
Ireland	1.0971	Turkey	482.70
Israel	6.91	USA	1.6140
Italy	2,730.0		

SOURCE: NATIONAL WESTMINSTER BANK

If the exchange rate increases (or *appreciates*), you will get more francs for the pound, so that they have become cheaper. If the exchange rate falls (or *depreciates*), you will get fewer francs, so that they have become more expensive.

From your personal point of view, when planning a trip abroad, if the pound appreciates, it is good news; but if it depreciates, it is bad news because you will get less foreign currency in exchange for your pounds. However, for the economy as a whole, the advantages and disadvantages of rising and falling exchange rates are far less clear cut.

Activities

1 A Jaguar car is sold for £25,000. What will be its price in the USA (the biggest market for Jaguars) at the following exchange rates?
  a £1 = $2.50
  b £1 = $2.00
  c £1 = $1.50
  d £1 = $1.00.

2 At which of the above exchange rates would American be most likely to buy Jaguars?

3 You go on holiday to France. Your hotel bill comes to 1,500 francs. If the exchange rates are:

a   £1 = FF 11
b   £1 = FF 10
c   £1 = FF 9
d   £1 = FF 8

how much money in pounds will you need in each case to change to pay your bill?

See p 117 at the back of the book for answers to these Activities.

HOW ARE EXCHANGE RATES DETERMINED?

The exchange rate is the price of a currency, and like all prices it is fixed by supply and demand. When the demand for the pound is high, it will cost a lot of Deutsche Marks or US dollars to buy. When demand for the pound is low, it will cost fewer Deutsche Marks or US dollars. Therefore, we must ask the question: what causes the demand for pounds to change? There are three main factors that decide the level of exchange rates.

First, if people in Germany wish to buy British goods, they will need British money. This is true whether they come here on holiday or whether they are buying the goods in Germany. While it is true that Germans can go to their local Horten or Kaufhof stores and pay for British-produced goods with their Marks, the company that bought the goods from a British supplier would have had to pay that manufacturer in pounds. Therefore, at the most fundamental level, it is the demand for a country's exports of goods and services that determines the demand for that country's currency and therefore determines the exchange rate.

Second, in the short run, other factors may influence the exchange rate. A high interest rate will encourage big financial institutions to save their money in your country where it will earn a high return. If foreigners wish to hold money in British bank accounts, they must first convert their money into pounds. The demand for pounds will thus rise, and so will the exchange rate – see the diagram at the top of page 73.

A major problem with using interest rates to keep the exchange rate high is that a high interest rate reduces the level of demand in the economy, and this leads to unemployment and low economic growth. In the long run, if the exchange rate is high because interest rates are high, then the financial institutions will become worried. They will know that a government will be tempted to cut interest rates if demand in the economy is low. However, once interest rates are reduced, there will then be less demand for pounds. The exchange rate will fall and each pound will buy fewer Deutsche Marks or US dollars. The savings will then not be worth as much. The sensible course of action will be to move the savings out before the pound reduces in value, but this action will lead to an increase in the supply of

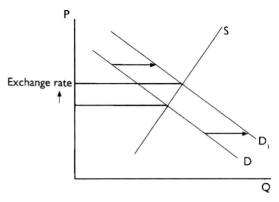

HOW AN INCREASE IN THE DEMAND FOR POUNDS LEADS TO A RISE IN THE EXCHANGE RATE FOR POUNDS

pounds and a fall in the exchange rate – see the diagram below. This is why, in the long run, a country's export position is more fundamental in determining the exchange rates than are interest rates.

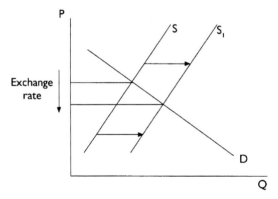

HOW AN INCREASE IN THE SUPPLY OF POUNDS LEADS TO A FALL IN THE EXCHANGE RATE FOR POUNDS

Third, speculators or foreign-currency dealers can help to influence the exchange rate in the short run. If you are a foreign-currency dealer and you think that the value of the pound is likely to fall, what is your best course of action? You would exchange your pounds for some other currency before the pound falls in value. However, other dealers will have the same information as you, and being sensible people they will sell their pounds also. There is now an increased supply of pounds, and so the exchange rate falls, proving to everyone that you took the correct course of action in selling your pounds. Now suppose you thought that the price of pounds would rise. What would be your sensible course of action? With all the other dealers, with the same information as you, again doing the same things, you would buy pounds while they are cheap and wait for the exchange rate to increase in line with the increased demand for pounds. And in this way, once again, the dealers have taken the best action.

In the short term, currency dealers can determine the price of a currency by their buying and selling decisions, but if firms need more pounds to buy more British products, then they will demand these and so increase the exchange rate. So again we are back to the fact that it is a country's international trade position that, in the long run, determines the value of the currency. Indeed, we have discussed the expectations of foreign-currency dealers, but what is it that leads them to believe that demand for a currency is likely to rise or fall? It is precisely their own expectations of what will happen to interest rates and exports.

Activity

What is likely to happen to the exchange rate for the pound against the Deutsche Mark in each of the following situations?

1   Volkswagen produces a new car that is highly desirable, very reliable and rather cheap.
2   Germany raises its rate of interest.
3   The English Tourist Board carries out a highly successful advertising campaign in Germany.

See p 118 at the back of the book for answers to this Activity.

THE EFFECTS OF EXCHANGE-RATE CHANGES

When the value of a currency falls or *devalues*, this means that you can exchange it for less of another country's currency. For example, in August 1998, £1 could be exchanged for around 2.8 Deutsche Marks. In August 1993, £1 would only buy about 2.3 Deutsche Marks. What difference does this make? The most obvious difference to individuals in Britain was for anyone going on holiday to Germany. A hotel room costing 100 Marks a night would have cost £35.71 in August 1998, but in August 1993, the same room at the same price in Marks would have cost £43.48.

Changes in exchange rates have a very real effect not just on individuals. A company that is importing or exporting may be dealing in thousands or millions of pounds. If the pound falls in value by 10 per cent then, faced with a bill for imports of £1,000,000, such a company will now have to add an extra £100,000 to its bill. Therefore, if the pound depreciates, imports become more expensive. This will increase prices in the economy and increase inflation. Exports then become cheaper in foreign markets, and so more will be bought, resulting in extra demand for British products and possibly a fall in unemployment.

A rise in the exchange rate will have the opposite effect. So, will a fall in the exchange rate be good for our international trade position? Not necessarily. A price rise will reduce demand, but by how much? What would happen to revenue if a 20-per-cent price increase resulted in only a 20-per-cent fall in the quantity demanded? The Marshall Lerner Condition says that it depends on how responsive to changes in price people are. The price of Japanese cars may increase, but people may nonetheless carry on buying them. Similarly, the price of British exports may fall, but if people are convinced that they are rubbish, they will not buy them.

UK car manufacturer Rover says it will halt production at its Longbridge plant in Birmingham on December 14.

The move raises fears of further job losses at the group but unions say they would take 'pragmatic approach' to the crisis.

Rover Chairman, Walter Hasselkus, said in a statement: 'The continued deterioration in some international markets, together with the challenges imposed by an over-valued currency, particularly on UK competitiveness, have caused us to take these actions.'

BBC News, 1 October 1998

A ROVER CAR

In 1998, the Bank of England was setting an interest rate of 7.5 per cent to keep down British inflation. As this was higher than in any other major Western country, money flowed into British financial institutions to benefit from these attractive interest rates. This increased the demand for pounds and led to an exchange rate of £1 = DM2.8. This made our exports uncompetitive.

FIXED AND FLOATING EXCHANGE RATES

Although the main influences on exchange rates are supply and demand, governments too can influence the value of a currency. At its extreme, this involves deciding on a value and then adopting measures to keep the currency at that level. How is this done? Earlier in this chapter, we saw that, fundamentally, an exchange rate is determined by the level of demand in foreign countries for a country's goods and services. Governments find it difficult to influence this. However, we also saw that the exchange rate can be influenced by interest rates: raising the interest rate will generally increase the demand for a currency and therefore increase its price.

From time to time, governments have entered into agreements where they are obliged to adopt measures that will keep the value of their currency at a particular level: a **fixed exchange rate**. The advantage of a fixed exchange rate is that businesses can make predictions about the prices of both their imports (for buying raw materials) and their exports (for sales). This is very important as a company importing cars will have to pay more for the imports if the currency depreciates, ie falls in value. The company will then try to pass these increased costs on to its customers by increasing prices. This will reduce the company's sales and therefore its profits. So, an importer loses out if the currency depreciates. Exporters will gain, however, as their products will be cheaper in the foreign market and so their sales will increase. However, an appreciation of the currency, ie an increase in its value, will have the opposite effects for exporters. Therefore, businesses generally prefer the exchange rate to remain stable.

One disadvantage of fixed exchange rates is that a country may need to run a high interest rate, making borrowing very expensive and discouraging investment, in order to keep the exchange rate fixed.

The alternative is to allow the exchange rate to float; ie here the government does not worry about the exchange rate when choosing policies. A currency may be left completely free to find its price on the basis of supply and demand in the market. This is called *clean floating*. Usually, however, a government will take some interest in the value of a currency, if only to stop large fluctuations from day to day. It may intervene by using the central bank to buy or sell pounds. This is known as a *managed float* or *dirty floating*.

Activity
The advantages and disadvantages of a **floating exchange rate** are the opposite to those for a fixed rate. Can you say what they are?

THE EUROPEAN MONETARY SYSTEM

The diagram below shows that the pound is becoming more expensive in terms of other currencies, and so are our exports. The ECU is the European Currency Unit and is an average of all the exchange rates of the different European Union currencies.

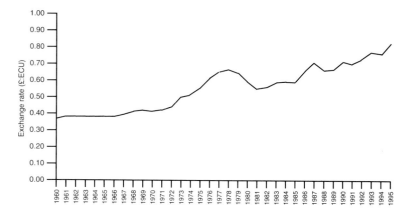

How much a pound costs in ECUs
SOURCE: EUROSTAT

From 1972 until 1990, Britain had a floating exchange rate which was managed from day to day by the Bank of England.

In 1979, the European Community (EC) member countries established the European Monetary System (EMS) and its Exchange Rate Mechanism (ERM). Britain did not join the ERM until 1990, and then at a high exchange rate. It came out in September 1992 because of speculation by foreign-currency dealers. When the pound began floating again, it depreciated sharply, and this made it easier for British firms to export.

The ERM is a *semi-fixed* exchange-rate system. In a fixed system, governments agree to adopt policies that will keep their currencies 'pegged' to a specific exchange rate against other currencies. In the ERM, a currency only has to stay within a certain band around a fixed point. It can thus fluctuate around that fixed point (for Britain from 1990 to 1992, by 6 per cent either way), but if the currency goes too high, the government must take action to reduce its value, and if it goes too low, it must take action to increase its value.

BLACK WEDNESDAY

The main problem with fixing your exchange rate to the currency of another country is that an important factor in deciding the exchange rate is the level of interest rates. If interest rates were all the same, then financial institutions would rather keep their money in a country with a record of low inflation so that it would maintain its value. Britain does not have a record of low inflation, and so to persuade financial institutions to keep money in Britain, a higher rate of interest must be offered than that in, say, Germany.

Throughout the summer of 1992, it was reported that the interest rates needed to maintain the exchange rate of the pound against the Deutsche Mark were far too high because Britain was suffering a recession while Germany's problem was inflation. On Wednesday 17 September, foreign-currency dealers began to sell pounds in the expectation that interest rates would soon have to fall. The Bank of England, assisted by other European Central Banks, sold its currency reserves to buy pounds. However, pounds were being sold more quickly than they could be bought. This continued until 11 am when the Bank of England announced that it would raise interest rates from 10 per cent to 12 per cent. Nobody believed that this would last, and the pound continued to be sold. At 2.15 pm, the interest rate was raised to 15 per cent, and when even this didn't work, the government announced that the pound was leaving the ERM.

In the next few weeks, the exchange rate fell by around 20 per cent against the Mark, and over the next few months interest rates were reduced by 6 per cent. The depreciation of the pound led to increased demand for British exports, while the fall in interest rates led to increased demand in the British home market.

Activity

So, was it 'Black Wednesday' after all? What do you think? Some people now refer to it as 'White Wednesday'.

Divide a page into two columns. In the left-hand column, put a heading 'Black Wednesday'. In the right, write 'White Wednesday'. Under 'Black Wednesday' write all the disadvantages you can think of connected with Britain's withdrawal from the ERM. Under 'White Wednesday', list all the advantages that have come about.

ANTI-TORY 'HURRICANE' RUINS HOPE OF REVIVAL

Professor Anthony King after the first by-elections of the 1997 Parliament

It is often said that the people's political memories are short. In fact, the opposite is true. Precisely because most people are interested only marginally in politics, they form views of the major parties that long outlive the events that gave rise to them.

The Tories under both Mrs Thatcher and Mr Major in 1992 successfully played on folk memories of industrial and financial chaos under Labour governments – chaos going back not just to the 1970s but to 1931, 1949 and 1967.

The Tories' problem now is that their image since the 1992 election has become a compound – one that looks like enduring – of Black Wednesday, broken promises, soaring interest rates, overcrowded hospitals, late-running trains and the former MP for Tatton.

Daily Telegraph, *22 November 1997*

SUMMARY

As with many political views on economic management, differences between Conservative and Labour thinking in the 1980s have transformed into general agreement in the late 1990s. While the free-market beliefs of 1980s Conservatives insisted on free trade with the rest of the world, the Labour policy of the early 1980s favoured a degree of protectionism. This had been abandoned by the 1990s, and there was a free-trade consensus between the parties, with Britain's entry into the Exchange Rate Mechanism (ERM) receiving cross-party support.

The value of the pound against other currencies has been consistently falling over the last 20 years. This makes imports dearer and British exports cheaper, thus helping the British balance of payments. However, in October 1998 Prime Minister Blair declared that this policy could not continue indefinitely. A falling exchange rate protects domestic industry from the consequences of international competition. However, it also raises the price of imports which may be raw materials and has the direct consequence, for British residents travelling abroad, that they receive less foreign currency to spend for every pound they exchange.

Revision Hints

The content of this chapter will mainly be appropriate for contributing to answers about the changing role of the state in the management of the economy. The most obvious example of this change is in exchange-rate policy where the floating exchange rate was managed by Nigel Lawson in the mid-1980s, and where subsequently, during the British membership of the ERM, the government was obliged to set interest rates to maintain the pound's parity against the Deutsche Mark. 1992 saw a return to free floating, accompanied by the then Chancellor of the Exchequer Norman Lamont singing in his bath to celebrate the liberation of no longer having to manage interest rates to maintain the pound's value.

The potential of the single currency is a related topic, and is dealt with in the next chapter.

Exam Hints

For the most part, this chapter needs to be considered alongside the next chapter. However, questions are asked about the political significance of Black Wednesday, and so the passage by Anthony King on page 79 is important. The political significance of economic events can be long lasting. The 1978/79 Winter of Discontent effect worked against the Labour Party for many years, and it is likely that Black Wednesday similarly altered the public perception of the Conservative's ability to manage the economy for a long period. Throughout the 1980s and 1990s, Conservative governments were elected not on the basis of popular policies (Labour policies were often more popular) but on a public belief in the Conservative's ability to manage the economy. This confidence was shattered by Black Wednesday.

Practice Questions

1 What was the political significance of Black Wednesday (September 1992)?
2 'The exchange rate has mirrored government acceptance of Britain's economic decline.' Discuss.
3 In what sense was Black Wednesday (17 September 1992) the Conservative Winter of Discontent?

8

THE EUROPEAN UNION

Introduction

IN THIS CHAPTER, we will see how the European Economic Community has grown in membership from six countries to fifteen; and in importance, taking on more powers, and becoming the European Union. We will examine the differences between a free-trade area and a 'common' or 'single' market (which, at least in principle, now exists in the EU), and we will consider how decisions are made in the EU. Finally, we will examine what is perhaps the most important economic and political issue facing Britain: whether to participate in the single currency.

Key Points:
- The birth of the European Union.
- A free-trade area.
- Britain and the EU.
- The institutions of the EU.
- The aims of the EU.
- Criticisms of the EU.
- Future developments.
- A single currency for Europe?
- Policy on Europe at the 1997 General Election.

THE BIRTH OF THE EUROPEAN UNION

In 1957, six countries (France, West Germany, Italy, Belgium, Luxembourg and the Netherlands) signed the Treaty of Rome which set out a programme to reduce the following hindrances to free trade in Europe:

- the imposition of tariffs and the restricted movement of goods;
- the inability of workers to move freely to jobs in other countries;
- restrictions on selling services;
- restrictions on the free movement of capital;
- the distortion of competition;
- the differences in laws which prevent a common market;
- the varying levels of taxes such as VAT.

By 1968, the **free-trade area** had established a customs union, but it took until January 1993 for a Single Market to be proclaimed. In the meantime, the original six countries had been joined by Denmark, Ireland and Britain (in 1973), Greece (in 1981) and Portugal and Spain (in 1986). Austria, Sweden and Finland were to join in 1995.

In 1992, the **Maastricht Treaty** changed the European Community to the European Union (EU) of which all nationals of the member states became citizens. The Treaty also set out a timetable to achieve a single currency by the end of the century, and this began on 1 January 1999 in 11 countries.

The EU came into official existence on 1 November 1993 following the coming into force of the Maastricht Treaty, but with most countries still unsure of what it should be called. The EU officially extended the European Community (EC), which in turn was the more up-to-date name for the European Economic Community (EEC), itself an improvement on the original unofficial but more popular term the Common Market. The new Treaty made all Britons citizens of the Union as well as of Britain.

Activity
Does it make any difference to you whether the organisation is called the European Economic Community, the European Community or the European Union? Why does it matter to governments which term is used?

A FREE-TRADE AREA

This is created when a group of countries decides that there should be no trade barriers (eg tariffs or quotas) between them. They do this so that they may all benefit from *free trade* and may each buy the most efficiently produced goods. They each maintain quotas and tariffs on goods coming from outside the free-trade area.

A CUSTOMS UNION

Suppose three countries, A, B and C, form a free-trade area. They each impose tariffs on imports from outside the area. In country A, the tariff on imports is 10 per cent. In country B it is 25 per cent and in country C it is 30 per cent. Country D is outside the free-trade area and wants to sell something to somebody in country C. The sensible course of action for country D is to set up a company in country A, export to that company paying the 10 per cent tariff and then re-export to country C with no tariff charged. The effect is that country C gains no taxes while country A, with the lowest tariffs, gains all the tax that should go to country C. (See the diagram below.)

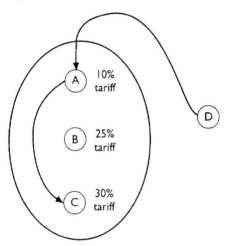

COUNTRY D'S STRATEGY FOR EXPORTING TO A FREE-TRADE AREA

To overcome this scenario, a common tariff would have to be agreed upon, but what should that tariff be, and how could it be changed? Each country would have to agree to giving up its right to set its own level of tax on imports, to a common body: a **customs union**. Therefore, each country would give up some of its sovereignty, ie the absolute right to make laws, to an institution made up of several countries.

A COMMON OR SINGLE MARKET

Even when a customs union exists, there are still other barriers to complete freedom of trade between members of a group. If the aim is to make it as easy to sell something made in one country to a person in another country as it is to sell something to someone in the original country, then other measures need to be implemented, such as the following:

- removing physical frontiers such as border checks on people and goods
- establishing common safety standards
- the recognition of the same professional qualifications in each country
- accepting tenders for contracts in the public sector from anywhere
- bringing together tax rates on goods
- common environmental policies.

BRITAIN AND THE EU

THE EUROPEANISATION PROCESS

The most important decisions the British government has had to take in the late 1990s are about its relationship with Europe. This is not just a matter of foreign policy, for such decisions will crucially affect Britain's own power and standing. What the government has to decide is how far it is prepared to become a constituent part of a European federation. In such a federation, a European government in Brussels, only partly elected from Britain, would decide British social policy, for example, and largely regulate the economy. Perhaps it may even direct foreign policy and deal with matters of peace and war involving British lives. Put this way, it seems as though the Conservative 'Eurosceptics' are right in claiming that British national sovereignty will disappear. They argue that British industry and finance will be constrained by European regulations, and that the achievements of the Thatcher period, such as the taming of trade unions, will be undermined by officials from Brussels. British competitiveness based on the availability of cheap labour will be eliminated by the imposition of European minimum standards, with the danger that investments will then go elsewhere. Eurosceptics see no benefits arising from these developments since their ideal is an independent British state regulating all its own internal and external affairs. Pro-Europeans, on the other hand, see the loss of autonomy as a price worth paying for the influence British governments and individuals can exert in a much larger political unit. Better to be part of a new superpower, they argue, than an independent but third-class state on the fringe of world developments. They point to the new opportunities available for finance and industry within the European Union (EU), and claim that British economic and social development will be faster and smoother within a more dynamic economy in which British financial expertise is joined with German industrial strength. The pro-Europeans believe that loss of political autonomy would be balanced by the British share in electing a European Parliament and government. European institutions would not be 'foreign' but representative of European citizens in Britain as much as they would be of European citizens in Spain, France, Italy, Scandinavia and the Low Countries.

If one thinks of the British Parliament and government, as Teresa Gorman and Margaret Thatcher do, as the sole bodies authorised to represent the British people, then one would regard a wider European democracy as threatening. However, many groups in Britain are positively attracted by Europeanisation. Scottish, Welsh and Irish nationalists see it as a way of easing the stranglehold of the British state on their own countries. The Labour Party and, in the 1990s, the Trades Union Congress (TUC) are reassured by the social protection the EU offers to vulnerable groups like low-paid workers. From the trade unions' point of view, undermining Thatcherite reforms might be no bad thing: employers' competitiveness is their employees' poverty.

Constitutional reformers see in the guarantees offered by the European treaties a protection for the civil liberties threatened by British governments. Even Conservatives like Kenneth Clarke, the former Chancellor of the Exchequer, see Europeanisation as a necessary step to consolidating Britain's world trading position rather than as a threat to it. These issues are not theoretical ones likely to affect us only in the next millennium for the EU already operates in Britain, parallel to but independently of the British government and Parliament. On a range of questions, British courts take their precedents from the European Court in Luxembourg, just as British civil servants and local councils follow directives from Brussels.

Relations between Britain and the EU are not a simple matter of 'us' and 'them'. This is because British MPs and civil servants participate in EU institutions and shape EU policy just as much as does any other national group. In fact, as one of the four leading member states in the EU, Britain plays a disproportionate part compared with most others. This was particularly true of the framing and implementation of the Single European Act (1986), with its free-market principles, which the ex-Conservative Commissioner Leon Brittan pushed through with the help of British economic advisers.

EU GRANTS AND REGULATIONS

Britain receives substantial grants from the European Regional Development Fund, created in 1975 to help poor or industrially run-down areas. Of the 50 million people in the EU living in such regions, 20 million are in Britain (Wales, Scotland, Northern Ireland and the North of England). The standard of living in Britain as a whole is almost exactly the EU average, but only in the south-east of England is it higher (by about 20 per cent), while in Northern Ireland it is 25 per cent lower. The special regions of Britain benefit from funds and policy initiatives aimed at building up small businesses and the tourist trade, retraining workers in declining agricultural areas, restructuring industry and retraining workers, rebuilding urban infrastructures and revitalising the economy in areas of industrial decline. Merseyside alone now receives about £1.3 billion from London and Brussels.

Common standards for the labelling and selling of foods have been adopted. Well-publicised examples in Britain involve the production of ice-cream, sausages and beer, but EU regulations cover a large proportion of the goods sold in shops. The EU has ruled that tobacco products must not be advertised on television, and it carefully regulates the amount and the timing of television advertising. Recently, it has also taken action to block British beef exports as a result of 'mad cow disease'.

COMMON AGRICULTURAL POLICY

As is so often the case, Britain's late entry into the European Economic Community – as it was called when Britain joined in 1973 – meant that policies had already been developed by others. At the end of the 1990s, a similar pattern is emerging with the creation of the single currency.

The Common Agricultural Policy (CAP) is the largest single item on the EU's annual budget, accounting for almost half the total, although it used to be three-quarters. It is intended to give some economic security to the large number of poor farmers and agricultural communities in Western Europe. This has involved higher farm prices and created the infamous 'wine lakes' and 'butter mountains'. Although British farmers benefit very substantially from CAP, the country as a whole pays more than it gets because British farms are relatively large and efficient. Currently, the EU's fishing policy is even more controversial because, in trying to preserve fish stocks, it has affected the livelihoods of fishing communities in Britain.

THE INSTITUTIONS OF THE EU

It has already been said that in order to make decisions which apply to all the member countries, special bodies need to be created. In the EU, the following institutions have been set up:

THE COUNCIL OF MINISTERS

This is the decision-making body of the EU. It is the only institution that can make laws. It consists of the relevant minister from each national government. So, if agriculture is being discussed, then the British Agriculture Minister attends, and when more general matters are being discussed, the Foreign Secretary attends.

At least once every six months, the heads of government meet to decide on major issues. The Council is chaired by each country in turn for six months. From January to June in 1998, Britain chaired all the meetings of the Council of Ministers, with Tony Blair hosting the heads of government in Cardiff.

THE COMMISSION

This is the civil-service body of the EU responsible for proposing ideas to the Council of Ministers and ensuring that the ministers' decisions are acted upon. The Commission is based in Brussels and is headed by a president who is chosen by the heads of government. Each government also appoints the Commissioners who head the various departments of the Commission. In 1998, Britain had two Commissioners, Sir Leon Brittan (a former Conservative Secretary of State) and Neil Kinnock (a former leader of the Labour Party).

Appointments of Commissioners are made by governments, but they must also be approved by the European Parliament. Commissioners promise to work for the joint interests of the whole EU rather than individual countries.

THE EUROPEAN PARLIAMENT

This is the only directly elected institution in the EU. Euro MPs (MEPs) are elected for five years, and they represent their local constituency and their political party rather than their country. Their power is quite limited, but the Parliament does have the right to reject the EU's budget and can reject the members of the Commission.

The Parliament is based in Brussels but holds its main meetings for one week a month in Strasbourg.

THE EUROPEAN PARLIAMENT

Do you know who is your local MEP (Member of the European Parliament)? Why not find out?

THE EUROPEAN COURT OF JUSTICE

This meets in The Hague, and its job is to ensure that European law is followed. It can punish, by fines, individuals, companies or governments. It is the highest court on all matters of EU law.

COURT BACKS DESIGNER LABELS IN DISCOUNT WAR

A new twist yesterday occurred in the long running battle between supermarkets and manufacturers of designer goods.

The decision by the European Court of Justice in Luxembourg was described by Consumer Affairs Minister Nigel Griffiths as 'bad news for consumers'. The Court ruled that trademark holders such as Adidas, Levi's, Calvin Klein etc can seek injunctions against retailers they believe to be selling unauthorised goods from outside the EU.

Adapted from The Guardian, *17 July 1998*

THE AIMS OF THE EU

The original objective of the EU was to increase the prosperity of its inhabitants by allowing them to get the benefits of the most efficient production in Europe, from wherever that may be. As always in economics, it is very difficult to know exactly how successful the EU has been in meeting its aim because we don't know what things would have been like if the EU had never existed. However, the *Lloyds Bank Bulletin* has estimated that Britain has experienced an extra 0.5 per cent of extra economic activity each year on average as a result of membership. Over time, the cumulative effect of this is very large, and this is largely due to the export market provided by membership.

CRITICISMS OF THE EU

Many people in Britain are very critical of the EU. Most accept the benefits of a free-trade area, but they worry about the EU being involved in social, regional and transport policy, monopolies and the environment. Since the first Customs Union, greater decision-making powers have been given up by national governments to Brussels. This has led to a reaction against the centralising power in Brussels and then to the adoption of the idea of *subsidiarity*, ie the idea that decisions should be made as close as possible to the area to which they apply; eg national government decides how much to spend on defence, while local government controls refuse collection.

FUTURE DEVELOPMENTS

The two most important future developments being discussed for the EU are:

1 enlargement to include the countries of Central and Eastern Europe
2 the development of the single currency which began on 1 January 1999 and which will be introduced gradually until 2002.

The newly democratised countries of Central and Eastern Europe, such as Hungary, the Czech Republic and Poland, are anxious to join, but they are a lot poorer than even the poorest of the existing members (Greece and Portugal). Having said that, the Czech Republic, Hungary and Poland have made great strides, and the EU has agreed in principle that they can join in the early years of the twenty-first century. Meanwhile, the single currency was introduced for 11 of the EU's 15 members on 1 January 1999, much to the anguish of many but by no means all British Conservative politicians.

A SINGLE CURRENCY FOR EUROPE?

On 1 January 1993, a Single Market was established throughout the European Community. However, many businesses would ask: how can you have a single market with many different currencies?

The aim of the Single Market was to make it as easy for someone in Manchester to buy a product produced in Milan as it is for someone in Los Angeles, California to buy something produced in Houston, Texas. However, Manchester uses pounds sterling and Milan uses Italian lire, while in both California and Texas the US dollar is a common currency.

If you go on holiday to another European country, you are faced with the problem of how to take foreign money. If you buy foreign currency from a bank, you will be charged commission. This is often around 2–5 per cent. Now imagine you are a business dealing in millions of pounds. Paying banks for foreign exchange can be very expensive. A single currency, the *euro*, would also solve the problem of the unpredictability of appreciations and depreciations discussed earlier.

However, who will control a single currency for Europe? In this country since 1997, the Monetary Committee of the Bank of England decides on the level of interest rates, ie on one interest rate that is the same in the south-east of England, in Scotland or in Cornwall. The problem here is often that while there may be a lot of demand in London (leading to inflation), at the same time the West Midlands may be suffering from a problem of *lack* of demand leading to unemployment. The Bank of England has to make an interest-rate decision that will affect both areas. The British Chancellor of the Exchequer gives the Bank of England an inflation target to aim for, and the Bank must use monetary policy to achieve this.

Could all the finance ministers of the EU get together to fix interest rates throughout Europe? This would make quick decisions almost impossible. The system adopted is rather like the German system of an independent central bank controlling European interest rates, with the governor of each country's own central bank (eg the Bundesbank in Germany) forming the council that will set a common interest rate for all countries in the single currency.

A problem might arise if one country is suffering from a lack of demand so that there is high unemployment, while another country has plenty of demand leading to inflation. Should European interest rates here go up or down?

BRITAIN AND THE SINGLE EUROPEAN CURRENCY

According to the British Treasury:

Even though the UK will not be joining the single currency on 1 January 1999, it will directly affect many UK businesses, especially those which buy and sell products throughout Europe. The euro will probably be used for doing some business within the UK itself, particularly in supply chains dealing with multinational companies. UK businesses therefore need to think now about how the euro might affect them and what they should do to prepare.

HM Treasury, Preparing for the Euro

The Treasury has issued advice for British businesses, advising them that they need to take account of the effects of the single currency on their business.

What will the euro mean for British business?

The single currency will sharpen competition throughout Europe, and it will influence the markets in three important ways:

1 *Cheaper transaction costs.* The single currency will remove the need to change currencies in cross-border trade within the euro zone. This will reduce (but not remove) transaction costs, making it cheaper for firms to make payments between countries in the euro zone. Firms in countries which join the euro will notice the greatest difference, but the effect will be felt by all businesses trading in the euro zone.

2 *exchange-rate certainty.* The single currency will remove uncertainties in exchange-rate movements for trade between countries in the euro zone. This will also remove the degree of protection from competition which these afforded.

Similarly, if product prices are set in euro, exchange-rate risks might be transferred to firms in countries outside the euro zone. Exchange-rate certainty may also lead to better business decision-making for those companies trading in the euro zone.

3 *transparent price differences.* The single currency will make price differences throughout the euro zone more obvious. This will sharpen competition.

Strategic issues

British businesses should consider the following issues when reviewing their strategies:

- *increased cross-border competition.* Businesses wanting to export into the euro zone may face a competitive disadvantage compared to firms throughout the euro zone which share the same currency as the importer.

- *cross-border mergers and other joint ventures.* Increased competition might make mergers with other businesses more likely, and sharing the euro would probably make them simpler.

- *distribution and purchasing.* The single currency might make distribution and purchasing arrangements simpler and cheaper since it would no longer be necessary to guard against exchange risk within the euro zone.

- *raising finance.* The range of options available to firms may increase since bond and equity (share) markets in euro may be more attractive.

- *market opportunities and threats.* The euro will bring new opportunities and threats for many businesses, especially – but not only – in countries in the euro zone. Firms will need to reconsider their marketing strategies, particularly pricing points where products are priced in euro.

Practical issues

If Britain were to join the single currency, every business in the country would be affected. In the meantime, while Britain remains outside the euro zone, the implications for a British business will depend on its sector of activity and amount of trade. For example, businesses with cross-border operations in continental Europe or with firms based in the euro zone might require practical changes. Businesses with purely local markets, customers and suppliers would probably not be affected. Here are some practical issues that British businesses might need to consider:

- *Financial systems and accounts.* British firms which keep accounts of dealings in other major European currencies would need to handle the euro, although other businesses' accounts may not be affected. Some firms may want to consider whether to change their accounting systems.

- *Business finance.* Firms, especially those with cross-border operations, will want to consider the financial services they require. Larger businesses, with internal treasury operations, will need to consider the effects of the European Monetary Union (EMU) on the financial markets, as well as on their own internal arrangements.
- *Pricing policy.* Companies exporting goods into the euro zone may have to decide whether to set new pricing points since prices quoted in national currencies are unlikely to convert into 'attractive' numbers in euro. They may also consider new pricing and packaging strategies – with manufacturing implications.
- *Information technology (IT).* There is no single solution to changing IT so as to handle the euro. For example, in some businesses, IT systems are linked, controlling accounts, stock, prices and payroll. In other, they are separate. Early evaluation will be important as the task may not be straightforward and resources may already be devoted to the Year 2000.
- *The status of the euro in Britain.* While Britain remains outside EMU, the euro will be a foreign currency in Britain and will not be legal tender. British businesses will not have to accept it unless they agree to do so. The government will facilitate the use of the euro in Britain where businesses wish to use it.

Source: HM Treasury

POLICY ON EUROPE AT THE 1997 GENERAL ELECTION

CONSERVATIVES

Europe was generally seen as the key issue splitting the Conservative Party. Although it saw Britain as one of several nation states rather than part of a European superstate, it was committed to Britain's membership of the EU.

The official Conservative policy on whether to join EMU in the first wave was not to rule it out but instead to announce a policy of 'wait and see'. However, if the Conservatives did decide to join the single currency within the course of the next Parliament, when they were committed to a referendum to confirm that decision.

The Party was also opposed to further moves towards federalism, although it did support a 'Partnership of Nations' and a further enlargement of the Union's membership. The Common Agricultural Policy was also seen as an area needing radical reform.

The Conservatives are extremely protective of Britain's veto in the key area of voting, and did not want to see this eroded, nor did they want any extension of Qualified Majority Voting (a system where countries are given a number of votes based on the size of their population, so that Germany has most votes, while

Luxembourg has the least). They also pledged to prevent any attempts to transfer powers from Westminster to the European Parliament or European Commission. In addition, the Conservatives wanted a solution to the problem of 'quota hopping' on the part of European fishermen.

They wanted to see the European Court of Justice reformed. Reforms here would include a time limit on the retrospective application of ECJ judgements, an internal appeals procedure, a limit on damages payable by member states found to be breaching Treaty obligations, and a national time limit on the implementation of directives. The party would not sign up to the Social Chapter.

LABOUR

Despite having its own internal splits, Labour promised not be be isolated and left behind in Europe. It would retain Britain's veto in matters of national interest but would relax it and allow Qualified Majority Voting to be extended in other areas. Although the party supports progress to EMU and a single currency, entry would only come after both a look at its economic practicalities and a referendum.

Labour also wanted the convergence criteria laid down in the Maastricht Treaty to be extended to cover jobs and productivity. Gordon Brown has also revealed five British tests on which Britain's entry to the EMU depend: whether European countries are at a different stage of the economic cycle; whether there is sufficient flexibility in the operation of the new currency's stability pact and in labour markets to respond to shocks; whether employment levels would suffer; the impact on investment by British companies here and on the Continent; and the impact on the British financial-services industry.

Since the 1997 General Election, the Labour government has signed up to the Social Chapter of the Maastricht Treaty, thus putting British employees on the same footing for working conditions as those in the rest of the EU.

Labour also said that it wanted to build alliances with those in the EU who share its views, and that it wanted urgent action and reform in the following areas: unemployment, Common Agricultural Policy, Common Fisheries Policy, greater openness in EU institutions and a more vigorous approach to the Single Market. Labour also supported the enlargement of the Union, with countries willing and able to join being offered membership.

Labour proposed to extend the Single Market to new sectors such as energy, telecommunications and biotechnology to create opportunities and benefits for consumers and to ensure that business is able to compete on a level playing field. The party would also establish a European Recovery Fund to promote investment, create jobs and boost growth.

LIBERAL DEMOCRATS

The Liberal Democrats were the most pro-European of the three major parties, although they were also the first to propose a referendum on the single currency.

They considered the reform and extension of Qualitative Majority Voting (QMV) to be imperative. This extension would see QMV cover all policy areas except constitutional matters (such as enlargement and Treaty amendment), the EU's financing system, its overall budget ceiling and the deployment of troops. They also wanted to see further development in EMU, which they believed Britain should have a greater role in than at present.

They also supported expanding the law-making role of the European Parliament, involving it in legislative areas where QMV applies and in the Council of Ministers, and they also supported increasing its scrutiny of Brussels bureaucrats. They were keen for greater co-operation on Common Foreign and Security Policy, and to incorporate the Western European Union (a defence and security association which includes all the European members of NATO) in the long term.

The introduction of a European Central Bank was also supported by the Liberal Democrats.

THE PARTIES AND THE SINGLE CURRENCY

The present Labour government has started to make positive sounds about joining the single currency, and 2002 looks like a likely date. Although the single currency officially began on 1 January 1999, when the 11 member countries locked together their exchange rates and the European Central Bank became responsible for their interest rates, euro notes and coins will actually only begin circulating in 2002.

The Liberal Democrats favour entry as early as possible but after a referendum. They call for a clear commitment to join, and they argue that this would encourage the exchange rate to fall as currency speculators realise that Britain too is to join the euro.

The Conservatives have become noticeably more Eurosceptic since the election, with the avowedly Eurosceptic William Hague narrowly defeating the pro-European Kenneth Clarke for leadership of the party. William Hague spent the year to October 1998 pushing his party to an anti-single-currency position, one now adopted by the Party much to the regret of leading Conservatives such as Clarke and former Deputy Prime Minister Michael Heseltine.

Conservative leader William Hague has won the overwhelming backing of his party for his anti-single currency policy. Party members supported by 170,558 votes to 31,000 Mr Hague's policy of ruling out joining the euro for the duration of this and the next Parliament.

This represented a Yes vote of 84.4 per cent, against 15.6 per cent who voted No – a victory margin of more than five to one.

Former Deputy Prime Minister Michael Heseltine commented:

'Every time we take one of these euro-sceptic lurches, it actually coincides with a reduction in popular support. The party must not move further to the right.' The leadership's policy, he said, was 'a step away from traditional Tory policies of pragmatism. Every Conservative prime minister I have worked for, Macmillan, Douglas-Home, Heath, Thatcher and Major, all those people in government, when faced with the decisions, took us further and further into Europe.'

BBC News, 5 October 1998

SUMMARY

- In 1998 the European Union (EU) comprised France, Germany, Italy, the UK, the Netherlands, Belgium, Luxembourg, Denmark, Greece, Spain, Portugal, Ireland, Austria, Sweden and Finland.
- The EU has eradicated trade barriers between member states and has introduced the free movement of people, goods and money between its members.
- The EU is run by institutions which contain representatives of each country but which work for the interests of the whole Union.
- Many people worry about the loss of sovereignty, ie the right of the British Parliament to make any laws it wishes, as more power is given to EU institutions.

STUDY GUIDES

Revision Hints

On the one hand, the topic of the EU stands as a discrete political issue all on its own. On the other hand, the EU has a major impact on British economic policy, with the issue of whether or not to join the single currency being the greatest economic choice facing any British government. The issue of the EU is one that has run through all the parties. In the 1960s, the Labour government showed an interest in joining, but it was Sir Edward Heath's Conservative government that negotiated Britain's entry. By then, a sizeable chunk of the Labour Party was anti-EEC, believing it to be a capitalist club working against the interests of the workers. However, in 1975 the Labour government held a referendum recommending that Britain stay in. Two-thirds of voters supported this proposition, despite several labour Cabinet Ministers urging withdrawal.

There were also splits within the Conservative Party, with the nationalist element led by Enoch Powell wanting nothing to do with the EEC. Margaret Thatcher was sympathetic to this position but recognised that British business needed the advantages of free trade that EU membership brought. Meanwhile, under Neil Kinnock's leadership in the 1980s, the Labour Party took on the enthusiasm of the convert, seeing the EU as favouring the worker against the interests of policies of Thatcherite deregulation.

Exam Hints

Questions concentrate on party policy on the EU, and this is very complicated. The key issues are that business is pro-EU because of the trade advantages, while both Conservative and Labour policies, on the other hand, have changed. Will the Conservatives' changing position lead to their break up? Can the pro-business, pro-Euro faction of Clarke and Heseltine stay in the party of English nationalism?

Practice Questions

1 Distinguish between Conservative and Labour policies on the European Union.
2 Discuss the impact of the European Union on British party politics.

9

THE THIRD WAY

Introduction

IN THIS CHAPTER, we will examine the significant economic policy changes brought about by the election of the 'New' Labour government in 1997. We will see how within days of coming to power, the government gave to the Bank of England the main tool for managing economic policy in the short term, while announcing that it itself would concentrate its attention on long-term issues (what economists call the supply side, while the Bank of England now manages the demand side of the economy). We shall see that this fundamental move was made for sound reasons, although Conservatives criticise the decision. We shall go on to discover how the 'Third Way' could be said to be traditional rightwing Labour policy now that the traditional leftwing has been marginalised.

Key Points
- The background, and a definition.
- Operational independence for the Bank of England.
- Welfare to Work.
- Welfare reform.
- The public-spending review.

THE BACKGROUND, AND A DEFINITION

During the early 1980s, while Thatcherism, advocating the rub of free-market forces, was in the ascendancy, the Labour Party was adopting increasing socialist ideas of economic control. In 1994, Tony Blair became leader of the Labour Party (after the sudden and unexpected death of John Smith) and set about radically reforming both the structures and the policies of the Party. Many people suspected that he didn't believe in anything other than winning the General Election. It is certainly true that he persuaded the party to drop electorally unpopular policies (a process that had begun as far back as 1983 under Neil Kinnock's leadership).

One of the battles fought by Blair was the dropping of Clause 4 from the Labour Party constitution. (See Chapter 4.) The Party was no longer interested in nationalisation following the perceived popularity of privatisation under the Thatcher government, even if this latter policy had turned distinctly unpopular under John Major. Indeed, the Labour government, as already mentioned, is now considering further privatisations of its own.

So, if Labour no longer represented socialism with mass nationalisation, was it simply a Tory party with a sweeter face? Labour under Tony Blair was in search of an ideology.

Before the 1997 election, Blair talked a lot about 'stakeholding', an important concept in business studies. This is the idea that a business has responsibilities to a number of different groups, only one of which is its shareholders. Employees, customers and the community in which it operates all have a stake in the actions of a business. In political literature, this is a subject that has been popularised in Will Hutton's book *The State We're In* which became a best seller shortly before the election. However, Hutton's prescription went too far for Blair.

Will Hutton calls for an interventionist government economic policy, with the government directing. However 'New Labour' believes in the government staying out of the running of the economy, so the search was on for an alternative ideology. In the USA, President Clinton talks about 'triangulation': the idea that policies could rise above the traditional battle between left and right. 'New Labour' prefers to call it the 'Third Way', a new politics that is neither conventional socialism nor free-market Thatcherism. The Third Way combines an acceptance of the current economic system with a desire for a fairer society. There are many who would argue that this idea is nothing new. Take, for example, some earlier policies of the rightwing of the Labour Party, including both those of Dennis Healey, who stayed with the Party after 1981, and those of Shirley Williams who left to form the Social Democratic Party which then merged with the Liberal Party to form the Liberal Democrats. Lord Rogers (formerly as a Labour Cabinet Minister Bill Rogers), leader of the Liberal Democrats in the House of Lords, has himself argued this point, but other commentators believe that at the heart of the Third Way does lie a new notion, namely of 'rights and responsibilities'. This has particular resonance in the field of welfare reform, but it also goes further, concentrating on the values of community with the state and encouraging active citizens to take initiatives themselves. On the other hand, Paddy Ashdown (the Liberal Democrat leader in 1998) talked about 'the enabling state'.

By October 1998, it was difficult to come to a conclusion as to the philosophical nature of the Third Way, but clues may be found in New Labour's first 18 months in government. The main themes of government economic policy since May 1997 have been:

- operational independence for the Bank of England
- 'Welfare to Work'
- welfare reform
- a public-spending review

and, standing in the background to all of this, the big issue of the single currency referred to in the last chapter.

OPERATIONAL INDEPENDENCE FOR THE BANK OF ENGLAND

This move has had far-reaching and fundamental consequences. The Chancellor of the Exchequer has in effect handed monetary policy over to the Bank of England. It is important to realise why he did this. After the Second World War, the Allies – notably Britain and the USA – were anxious that there should be a free and independent Germany, or at least West Germany, with strong and stable institutions. One of the problems that had led to the rise of Hitler was the hyperinflation of the Weimar Republic. To ensure that inflation did not become problematic in the future, an independent Bundesbank (or Central Bank) was given the task in the constitution of keeping down inflation. Everyone knew that if wage rises got out of hand, the Bundesbank would keep the money supply tightly limited, even though, with only a fixed amount of money to go around, unemployment would then rise. Similarly, no government in Germany could increase aggregate demand without the Bundesbank increasing interest rates to bring aggregate demand back down. As people knew this, they behaved accordingly, and until the time of German reunification, West Germany had a very stable economy.

The general trend in German unemployment has been upwards, but as the diagram at the top of page 100 shows, this really took off following reunification.

By contrast, in Britain, interest rates had been set by the Chancellor, latterly in collaboration with the Governor of the Bank of England but with the Chancellor having the last word. This resulted in what is now perceived as Conservative Chancellor Nigel Lawson's artificial boom of the late 1980s, initiated in order to bask in political popularity. In early 1997, the then Conservative Chancellor Kenneth Clarke refused the advice of Bank of England Governor Eddie George to raise interest rates to head off the prospect of inflation because it was just too near an election!

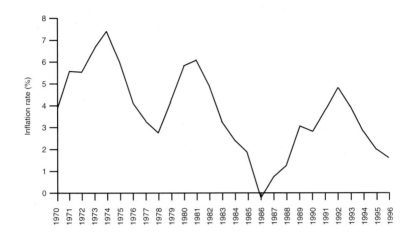

WEST GERMAN INFLATION RATES (PERCENTAGE)
SOURCE: EUROSTAT

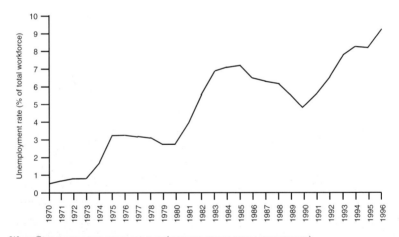

WEST GERMAN UNEMPLOYMENT RATES (PERCENTAGE OF TOTAL WORKFORCE)
SOURCE: EUROSTAT

The Labour Chancellor Gordon Brown now hopes that by setting an inflation target of 2.5 per cent and instructing the Monetary Committee of the Bank of England to achieve this by setting appropriate interest rates, he will be able to convince people that the policy is free of political interference.

By the summer of 1998, however, problems have been evident. The Bank of England believed that to achieve its inflation target, an interest rate of 7.5 per cent was needed. As this was higher than the general level of interest rates in the world, it proved attractive to savers, and so the value of the pound rose. In the summer of 1998, it was estimated that the pound was overvalued by around 30 per cent; in other words, you could buy a set of goods from a supermarket in, say, Lille in France for 30 per cent less than in, say, Ashford in Kent if you travelled through the Channel Tunnel. Orders for British exports died, and business leaders and unions demanded that the government do something. But the government could do nothing. The Bank of England had no remit to look at the exchange rate or unemployment, but only to achieve 2.5 per cent inflation, and so it too could do nothing. Tony Blair and Gordon Brown, however, argued that the short-term pain was worth the long-term gain. Meanwhile, Eddie George rejected trade-union demands to slash interest rates, saying such measures would only store up long-term problems for the future. Speaking at the 1998 TUC Conference (the first Governor of the Bank of England ever to do so), he pledged to bring rates down only if inflation fell below the government's target level:

In anything other than the short term [a reduction in interest rates] will be likely to mean more rather than less economic damage. And lower rather than higher growth and employment.

BBC News, October 1998

LABOUR'S PRIME MINISTER TONY BLAIR AND CHANCELLOR OF THE EXCHEQUER GORDON BROWN

WELFARE TO WORK

So, if the government has said that it will not use fiscal policy to manage aggregate demand, and it is leaving monetary policy to the Bank of England which is charged with targeting the rate of inflation to the exclusion of all else, does the government have any view on unemployment? Gordon Brown's answer is 'Welfare to Work' as this Treasury release makes clear:

WELFARE TO WORK

A package of measures to promote employability, invest in skills and move people from Welfare to Work were announced by the Chancellor today.

They provide a New Deal for:

- young people unemployed for more than six months
- the long-term unemployed
- lone parents
- schools.

These policy announcements mark the first step towards creating a welfare system fit for the next century and raising skill levels in the economy. The programmes for unemployed people will be of a high quality and focused on the needs of individuals, designed to ensure that on completion participants should not revert back to unemployment. The measures for lone parents will contribute to reducing the numbers dependent on benefits. The investment in schools will have the same effect for the future.

HM Treasury, 1997

Third Way principles dictate that rights, including in this case the right to do something productive, carry with them responsibilities, as the following extract demonstrates.

JOBLESS FACE BENEFITS CUT IN 'NEW DEAL'

By Jon Hibbs, Political Correspondent

The penalties for young people who refuse to take part in the Government's welfare-to-work programme will bite most heavily on single people aged 18–25 who are fit and living at home.

Unless they are sick, disabled or face mitigating personal circumstances, they face being penniless if they fail to take up either a subsidised job, work with a voluntary organisation, a place on an environmental task-force or full-time education.

If they refuse their case would be referred to an Employment Service adjudication officer with the prospect of losing all their weekly £38.90 Jobseekers' Allowance for a fortnight.

The Daily Telegraph, *4 July 1997*

The government is acting on the *supply side* of the labour market to make potential employees more employable by giving them both skills and experience of the world of work.

This is not new. The Youth Training Scheme of the 1980s tried something similar, but was criticised for its failure to deliver real training. The government believes that its new programmes will fit people for jobs where people are still needed because, ironically, although there is still high unemployment, there are some vacancies that go unfilled because employers cannot find people with the correct skills.

WELFARE REFORM

There will still be many people who will rely on welfare benefits for support. In the summer of 1998, Prime Minister Blair reaffirmed that welfare reform was a priority for his government. Mr Blair listed the government's achievement in this area, including those concerning the Child Support Agency, the New Deal for the unemployed and changes in lone-parent benefit, legal aid and asylum regulations.

The 1997 election result indicated the electorate's wish to embrace political change of a scale equal to, but radically different to that made by Mrs Thatcher.

On the Saturday after this election triumph I was offered the post of Minister for Welfare Reform. I sensed then only tentatively – but was to learn its full importance only later – that reforming welfare required a position of executive authority.

In the end I settled for a non-executive position wishing as I did, and still do, for the welfare reform programme to be the big success for which the country longs and to play some part in that revolution …

On the Monday after the election I talked with the Prime Minister about the welfare reform strategy. He gave his immediate agreement to the production of a Green Paper.

The idea was to produce a route map guiding how welfare reform should be conducted …

Over many years the Prime Minister has commented on my publications. There was much agreement on how welfare was impacting on people's lives, how it affected behaviour, how individuals saw, or did not see, their personal responsibilities and their duty to self-improvement.

Here then was the central theme of the welfare reform strategy. People's natural wish to improve their own lot and that of their families had to become once again the great engine force of social advance.

Much of current welfare expenditure counters this objective. And while the level of expenditure is an issue, the main concern is the cancerous impact that much of welfare has on people's motivation, their actions and thereby their character.

Extract from the speech by Frank Field MP, former Minister of State for Welfare Reform, following his sacking, 29 July 1998

Welfare reform has proved a political hot potato for all governments in the last 20 years. For most of the time since 1979, Labour attacked the Conservatives for meanness. Then, in 1995, Tony Blair promised to 'think the unthinkable' about welfare and at the election accused the Tories of spending too much. Yet, the problem is that while spending on social security in general is unpopular, the most expensive components are nonetheless politically impossible to cut.

Spending on old-age pensions soared under the Tories. In 1979, social-security spending amounted to 10 per cent of **gross domestic product (GDP)**. By 1997, it was over 12 per cent. Impervious to the efforts by ministers of all parties to catch its heels, it has been climbing ever since the modern welfare state was created by the Labour governments of 1945–51. The social-security bill has also risen sharply as a proportion of total government expenditure. This is probably the main reasons why, despite Tory pledges to roll back the frontiers of the state, public spending is about as large a slice of GDP as it was in 1979.

The Conservatives made several attempts to contain welfare spending. Perhaps the most significant of these was a decision in 1979 to make the basic state pension rise in line with prices rather than wages. Wages typically rise faster than prices, so this change saved the government a fortune. The pensions bill would have been 20 per cent higher in 1996 if pension increases were still based on average earnings.

Another big change to pension policy came in 1986 when the government encouraged workers to opt out of the state-earnings-related pension scheme (SERPS, which provides extra retirement income based on employees' contributions). Those who opted out received a subsidy that they were obliged to pay into either a company pension fund or a personal pension plan. Many who plumped for a personal pension were later found to have been ill-advised; some have been paid compensions by the firms that sold these pensions.

Another reform introduced by the Conservative government was the establishment of the Child Support Agency which aimed to save on state benefits paid to the children of divorced and separated couples. Its job was to track down parents who do not pay enough maintenance and make them pay more. Although the idea had all-party support, the Agency's first steps were unpopular and insensitive.

The Conservatives also replaced invalidity benefit with incapacity benefit which imposes a heavier burden of proof on anyone who claims to be medically unfit for work. Further, the new Jobseekers' Allowance tightened up unemployment benefit for everyone. It shortened the honeymoon period, during which a claimant's benefits do not depend on their means, from a year down to six months.

The use of *means-tested benefits* (ie benefits based on how much money you have) has grown hugely. In 1979, 2.9 million people received the main means-tested benefit; by 1995, 5.3 million did.

Old-age pensions and unemployment-related benefits remain major calls on public spending.

THE PUBLIC-SPENDING REVIEW

New Labour believes that one of the main obstacles to Labour's winning previous elections was the public's belief that the Party would put up taxes to finance higher public spending. At the election in 1992, public opinion polls showed that the public was in favour of greater spending on the National Health Service and on education, but Conservative posters sporting claims like 'Labour's double tax whammy' backed up by inaccurate stories about Labour's tax proposals in the rightwing press in the last few days of the campaign, led to an unexpected Conservative win.

To counter this, well before the 1997 campaign, New Labour committed itself to accepting the Conservative government's spending plans for the following two years, and promised no rises in income tax for anybody during the life of the Parliament (ie 5 years). Liberal Democrats attacked this stance, saying that it was pointless having Labour ministers implementing Conservative policies. However, Gordon Brown and Tony Blair believed it to be necessary to get elected.

In summer 1998, Gordon Brown announced the results of his Comprehensive Spending Review. While still constrained by the need to avoid tax increases, he was now free to spend on New Labour priorities, and as one might expect from New Labour, these happily coincide with what according to opinion polls are the public's favourites.

Our prudence has been for a purpose. It is because we have set tough efficiency targets, and reordered departmental budgets that our top priorities, health and education, will receive more new money than the other 19 Government departments combined. To accommodate this we have had to take a firm line with other spending programmes, and rigorously select priorities.

As a result more than half today's allocations – over 50 per cent – will be invested in health and education. So there will be additional resources – but it is money in return for modernisation.

Here the main conclusion of the Comprehensive Spending Review is that it is not just a social duty for government to invest in good public services, to improve our social fabric, and to tackle poverty and deprivation by extending opportunity. Most people in Britain, apart from a small and extreme minority, also agree that it is in the economic interests of the whole country to create an infrastructure of opportunity, and invest in education, science, transport and strong communities so that individuals can contribute to the economic and social well-being of the country.

In eighteen years of the last Government, spending on education rose on average by 1.4 per cent a year.

Education spending will now rise in real terms by an average of 5.1 per cent a year till the end of the Parliament.

We said we would devote a rising share of national income to education – and we have.

Spending on education will now rise to 5 per cent of national income.

The National Health Service is compassion in action, what its founder, Aneurin Bevan, rightly called the most civilised achievement of modern Government.

Under the last Government the increase for the last three years was 7 billion.

For the coming three years, I am announcing an increase in health service funding of a total of 21 billion.

Health department spending rose by an average of 2.5 per cent a year during the last Parliament. Next year it will rise by 5.7 per cent. The year after by 4.5 per cent.

For the rest of the Parliament this Government will achieve yearly real growth averaging 4.7 per cent.

Speech by Rt. Hon. Gordon Brown, Chancellor of the Exchequer

So, it would seem that the British remain obsessed with taxes and government spending. It is true that compared with the USA our taxes are high, but by European standards they are very low. Compare our tax rates with Denmark, for example – see the diagram at the top of page 107. Similarly, the level of government spending as a proportion of GDP is much higher in Denmark – see the diagram at the bottom of page 107.

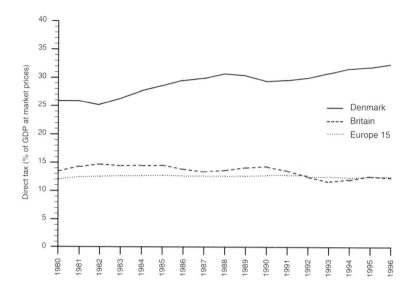

<small>D</small>IRECT TAXES AS A PERCENTAGE OF <small>GDP</small> AT MARKET PRICES
SOURCE: EUROSTAT

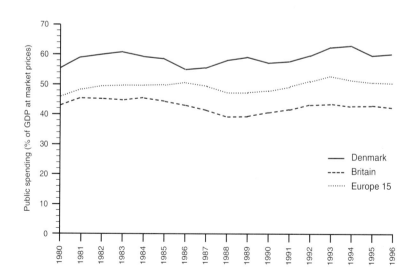

<small>T</small>OTAL GOVERNMENT EXPENDITURE AS A PERCENTAGE OF <small>GDP</small> AT MARKET PRICES
SOURCE: EUROSTAT

Revision Hints

This chapter has brought together the themes of this book. New Labour has tried to combine the social conscience of the traditional Labour Party with much of the free-market doctrine of Thatcherism; and the British government now plays a much less involved role in the economy than it did in the 1970s. Do not read this chapter in isolation, but try to trace through the themes from the beginning of the book and see how the emphasis of economic policy changes. As part of your revision, try to draw some time lines. At the end of the day, it is a balancing act, and the old problem is still with us: should the government concentrate on inflation or unemployment?

Exam Hints

Questions in the exam tend to ask for an overview of how an area of policy has changed over time. However, it is essential that you know the up-to-date position and can quote it in your essays. This will continue to evolve and change, and so you must keep up with developments via the media.

Practice Questions

1 '"New Labour" was a response to the success of Thatcherism.' Discuss.
2 How has the role of the state in the management of the economy changed since 1970?

GLOSSARY

aggregate demand   All the spending and investment in an economy, whether by individuals, business or government.

Budget (the)   The announcement by the Chancellor of the Exchequer of tax rates for the next financial year (beginning in April).

balance of payments   The record of all of the flows of money into and out of a country.

Chancellor of the Exchequer   The Cabinet Minister responsible for the running of the economy and for setting taxes and levels of government spending. The Minister in charge of Her Majesty's Treasury.

Common Agricultural Policy (CAP)   A European Union-wide policy for maintaining farmers' incomes.

customs union   An agreement between countries to levy no import duties on goods traded between them, on the one hand, and a uniform duty on imports from outside on the other.

cyclical unemployment   Unemployment brought about by a periodic downturn in the business cycle.

demerit goods   Goods whose consumption the government seeks to discourage by a ban or by tax – cigarettes being an obvious example.

denationalisation   The transfer of assets from the government to private individuals or businesses.

direct tax   Taxes levied directly on income; mainly income tax, but also corporation tax on companies.

duopoly   A situation where there are two major suppliers dominating the market.

elasticity of demand   A measurement of how much the quantity demanded will change as a result of any price change.

equilibrium   A state of balance in any economic situation.

exchange rate   The price of one currency expressed in terms of another. For example, if it costs 1.6 US Dollars to buy 1 pound sterling, the exchange rate is £1 = $1.6.

fiscal policy   Regulating demand by the use of government spending and taxes.

fixed exchange rate   An exchange rate that cannot be altered despite the pressures of supply and demand.

floating exchange rate   An exchange rate that is constantly shifting, reflecting supply and demand.

free-market economy   An economy where market forces are relatively free from government interference and where the government leaves the provision of goods and services to private businesses.

free-trade area   An agreement between countries neither to levy import duties nor impose quotas on goods traded between them.

frictional unemployment   Unemployment resulting from people moving between jobs.

gross domestic product (GDP)   The generally accepted measure of the value of all of a country's production of goods and services.

incomes policy   A policy that restricts pay rises and that can be applied to just the public sector (as in the 1990s) or across the whole economy (as tried in the 1970s).

income tax   A tax that is charged on the income earned by individuals.

indirect tax   Taxes on spending, such as VAT and excise duties on petrol, alcohol and cigarettes.

inflation   A rise in the general level of prices.

injection   An increase in demand brought about by an increase in investment, government spending or exports.

interest rates   The charge made for a loan, or the payment made for savings.

International Monetary Fund (IMF)   An international organisation that lends to governments in times of crisis in return for the governments' agreeing to adopt IMF policies in running their economy.

Keynes, John Maynard   The most famous British economist of the twentieth century, the father of postwar economics whose ideas were paramount between 1945 and 1975.

Keynesian economics   The school of economics which bases its thinking on the ideas of John Maynard Keynes and sees demand as the key to economic problems.

leakage   A reduction in demand brought about by an increase in savings, taxes or imports.

Maastricht Treaty   The treaty that changed the European Community into the European Union (EU), making everyone who is a citizen or subject of a member state a citizen also of the EU, providing minimum working standards and setting up the single currency.

macroeconomics   Economics which affect the whole country rather than just individuals and individual businesses.

mandate   The right of elected individuals to do something, based on the fact that the 'something' in question was known about at the election when people voted for them.

marginal cost pricing   Charging a price, per unit of output, that is just enough to cover the extra cost of supplying one extra unit of output.

merit goods   Goods and services (such as health and education) whose consumption is encouraged by the government by its providing them for free or at a low cost. These could also be provided by private businesses, in which case customers could be charged for them, but governments wish to spread their availability.

monetarism   The belief that inflation is caused purely by increases in the money supply beyond the economy's increase in output.

monetary policy   Regulating demand by the use of interest rates.

monopoly   A single supplier or producer who can dominate a market (in British law, this is defined as supplying at least one third of the market).

multiplier effect   The continuing effect of any initial increase in spending.

national insurance   A tax that is charged on the income earned by individuals that also acts as an insurance scheme allowing people who have made sufficient contributions to receive retirement pensions and Jobseeker's Allowance when needed.

nationalisation   The transfer of assets from private individuals or businesses to the government.

natural monopoly   A situation where it would not be feasible to have competing suppliers as the cost of replicating an infrastructure (eg pipelines or a national network of rails) would be prohibitive.

natural rate of unemployment   A level of unemployment that can be sustained without any inflationary pressure resulting.

neo-classical economics   The school of economics which looks back to traditional (prewar) views of economics and builds upon these to explain the present.

privatisation   A general movement from the public to the private sector, which may take many forms.

progressive tax   A tax that takes a greater proportion of the income of the better off.

proportional tax   A tax where everyone pays the same proportion of their income in tax, no matter how much they earn. It could be argued that **value-added tax (VAT)** is such a tax, as everyone here pays the same rate.

public goods   Goods, or, more likely, services, that can only be provided by the government as there would be no incentive for a private business to provide these; eg the armed forces.

Public Sector Borrowing Requirement (PSBR)   The government's need to borrow to fill the gap between tax revenue and government spending.

real prices   The difference between any particular price rise and the rate of inflation.

recession   Formally, a fall in national output for two successive quarters, ie over six months.

regressive tax   A tax that falls most heavily on the worse off.

Retail Prices Index (RPI)   A monthly measure of the price of a collection of goods and services representative of what people spend their money on.

seasonal unemployment   Unemployment at particular times of the year in specific occupations, due to the seasonal nature of the work.

slump   A severe and prolonged fall in economic activity.

stop–go economics   The policy of increasing demand to tackle unemployment only to quickly follow it with reducing demand to combat the resulting inflation.

structural unemployment   Unemployment that comes about through the decline of an industry.

subsidy   A payment by the government to reduce the price of something when it wishes to encourage consumption.

value-added tax (VAT)   The main tax on spending throughout the European Union.

wages councils   Bodies that used to set rates of pay for workers in traditionally low-paid jobs.

FURTHER READING

The following books will enable you to investigate further those topics that have been covered within this book.

A GENERAL TEXT:

Curwen, P. (ed) (1997) *Understanding the UK Economy*, London: Macmillan.

FOR ISSUES IN THE LANDMARK GENERAL ELECTION OF 1997:

Butler, D. and Kavanagh, D. (1997) *The British General Election of 1997*, London: Macmillan. This book is the 15th Nuffield election study, and provides a definitive account of the election, with statistics to assist.

BIBLIOGRAPHIES OF PEOPLE WHO WERE IMPORTANT IN TWENTIETH-CENTURY ECONOMIC POLICY:

Dell, E. (1997) *The Chancellors*, London: HarperCollins. An authoritative review of the impact of some important Chancellors of the Exchequer. Adds the personality to economic policy.

Friedman, M. and Friedman, R. (1998) *Two Lucky People: Memoirs*, Chicago: University of Chicago Press. The memoirs of the father and mother of monetarism, the economic policy that dominated the 1980s throughout the Western world.

Grigg, J. (1995) *Lloyd George*, London: HarperCollins. An important biography of the man who changed the whole role of government in the economy, first through welfare provision and then through direct intervention and management during the First World War.

Pym, H. (1998) *Gordon Brown*, London: Bloomsbury. What makes the Chancellor of the Exchequer tick? Get to know the man who runs the nation's economic policy with the help of one of the BBC's top policital journalists.

Young, H. (1993) *One of Us*, London: Pan Books. This biography of Margaret Thatcher is based on extensive interviews with the subject and colleagues who worked for her. It traces her life from being a junior minister under Macmillan to her hatred of all that the Conservatism of the 1950s and 1960s stood for, and her radical response.

FOR IMPORTANT THEORIES AND PRINCIPLES:

Blair, T. (1996) *New Britain – My Vision of a Young Country*, London: Fourth Estate. As Leader of the Opposition, Tony Blair here set out his vision. See for yourself whether he is now following this vision in government.

Evans, E. (1997) *Thatcher and Thatcherism*, London: Routledge. An inexpensive little book (160 pages) which surveys the origins and the impact of Thatcherism.

Galbraith, J.K. (1993) *The Culture of Contentment*, Harmondsworth: Penguin Books. A seminal work by one of the twentieth century's leading economic thinkers and critics of the system. He describes the modern phenomenon of the connected wealthy: a large class of people who have no interest in helping the poor and who will ensure that no government can be elected that seeks to significantly improve the lot of the poor.

Hutton, W. (1996) *The State We're In*, London: Vintage. A seminal work for New Labour while in opposition. Hutton analyses the problems of the British state and puts forward an agenda that many have seen as an intellectual foundation for the Third Way.

Hutton, W. (1997) *The State To Come*, London: Vintage. A personal manifesto from the author of the highly significant *The State We're In*, published just in time for the 1997 election. In government, New Labour has found Hutton's ideas rather too radical.

Marquand, D. (1999) *The Progressive Dilemma: From Lloyd George to Blair*, London: Fontana. David Marquand is one of Britain's leading thinkers in the social-democratic tradition, and in this book he traces the limits to reform of the economic and political system, limits which have operated throughout the century and were seen in the opposition to Lloyd George's historic creation of a rudimentary welfare system.

Marquand, D. and Seldon, A. (1996) *The Ideas That Shaped Post-war Britain*, London: Fontana. A collection of essays by some of Britain's leading political analysts on the evolution of politics and economics in Britain since the Second World War.

Marx, K. and Engels, F. (1970) *The Communist Manifesto*, London: Pathfinder. A reprint of the definitive nineteenth-century publication that laid the foundation for much of the economic organisation of the twentieth century.

Stewart, M. (1991) *Keynes and After*, Harmondsworth: Penguin Books. A look at the influence of Keynes and his ideas through the postwar period.

Steward, M. (1993) *Keynes in the 1990s*, Harmondsworth: Penguin. Keynesian economist Michael Stewart applies the principles of Keynes to the 1990s. In a sense, a sequel to *Keynes and After*.

Tam, H. (1998) *Communitarianism*, London: Macmillan. One of the key influences on the Third Way, this American idea is neither socialist nor free-market capitalist.

FOR COMMENTARIES ON RECENT ECONOMIC HISTORY:

Critchley, J. and Morrison, H. (1998) *Collapse of Stout Party*, London: Indigo. Based on a diary kept by the highly entertaining former Conservative MP Julian Critchley, this book charts the path of the Conservative Party since Margaret Thatcher left office in 1990.

FOR UNDERSTANDING ISSUES:

Goodman, S.F. (1996) *The European Union*, London: Macmillan. This book applies economic theory in a clear and direct manner to issues such as exchange rates, agriculture, international trade and monetary union.

Johnson, C. (1996) *In with the Euro, Out with the Pound*, Harmondsworth: Penguin Books. An affordable little book (272 pages) which sets out the facts in favour of the introduction of the euro and how in practice it would be implemented.

Layard, R. (1997) *What Labour Can Do*, London: Warner. One of Britain's leading economists, who has spent much of the 1990s advising the Russian government, turns his attention to advising the new Labour government, concentrating on what can rather than cannot be done.

Stephens, P. (1996) *Politcs and the Pound*, London: Macmillan. The pound has been a recurring problem in British politics throughout the twentieth century. Churchill's return to the gold standard, Wilson's forced devaluation and Major's entanglement with the ERM have all wrought political destruction for their parties. Now the pound represents the fault line in British politics as the government decides whether to get rid of the currency, and so the problem.

THE MEDIA

It is important to keep up to date by reading the quality press (ie *The Guardian, The Telegraph, The Times* and *The Independent*) and watching programmes such as *Newsnight* on BBC2 or *Channel 4 News*. Many current-affairs programmes occur during the week, so make sure you consult the *Radio Times* to plan for relevant programes. BBC Radio 4 is a wonderful resource.

If you only consult one publication mentioned in this further-reading section make it RADIO TIMES.

THE INTERNET

There are also some useful Internet sites. BizEd is an excellent starting point.

- BizEd = http://www.bized.ac.uk
- HM Treasury = http://www.hm-treasury.gov.uk

ANSWERS TO ACTIVITY QUESTIONS

Question 1, p 16:

1	a The Police	Public
	b The Navy	Public
	c The National Health Service	Merit
	d Clacton County High School	Merit
	e Chelmsford College of Further Education	Merit
	f The Fire Brigade	Public
	g The University of Brighton	Merit

All the merit goods can exclude people from their use quite easily. In Britain, we choose to provide health care and education free at point of use, but there are private hospitals and schools showing that you can exclude non-payers.

The Fire Brigade is an interesting example because, before local councils set up fire services, insurance companies would employ a fire brigade to put out fires as long as you had a policy with them. This was clearly impractical, however, as your insurance policy was not something you had a lot of time to look for while your house was burning down!

Question 2, p 38:

a denationalisation
b competitive tendering
c the sale of public-sector property
d deregulation.

Question 3, p 50:

1 5 per cent of £10 is 50p, so you would need £10.50 to give you the same spending power, assuming that your spending pattern matches the average spending pattern upon which the RPI is based (in practice, however, this is unlikely).

2 Prices never fell over the period shown. In 1989, they rose by 9 per cent, and in 1990 they only rose by 6 per cent but they still went up! They just went up less quickly. So, although the rate of inflation fell in 1988 and 1990, prices continued to rise.

Page 71–2:

1 a $62,500
   b $50,000
   c $37,500
   d $25,000
2 At the exchange rate of £1 = $1.00.

3 a £136.36
   b £150.00
   c £166.67
   d £187.50

Page 74:

1 The exchange rate will fall: as British and German people switch from buying British cars to buying the Volkswagen instead, the demand for pounds will fall, and so therefore will the exchange rate for the pound.
2 The exchange rate will fall: as more pounds are converted into Deutsche Marks and saved in German bank accounts at this more attractive rate of interest, the demand for pounds falls, and so therefore will the exchange rate for the pound.
3 The exchange rate will rise: as more Germans come over to spend their money on British goods and services, the demand for pounds will rise, and so therefore will the exchange rate for the pound.

INDEX

ACCESS TO POLITICS

Access to Politics is a series of concise and readable topic books for politics students. Each book provides advice on note taking, tackling exam questions, developing skills of analysis, evaluation and presentation, and reading around the subject.

TITLES PUBLISHED IN 1998:

UK Government and Politics in Context	0340 71134 5
Protecting Rights in Britain	0340 71136 1
Local and Regional Government in Britain	0340 71184 1
Voting Behaviour and Electoral Systems	0340 71135 3
British Politics and Europe	0340 72079 4

TITLES PUBLISHED IN 1999:

The Prime Minister and Cabinet Government	0340 74759 5
Pressure Groups	0340 74758 7
The Environment and British Politics	0340 74791 9
The Government and the Economy	0340 74278 X
Law, Order and the Judiciary	0340 75772 8

See page iv for information on how to order copies.